UNDERSTANDING

MICHAEL
PORTER

JOAN MAGRETTA

UNDERSTANDING

MICHAEL PORTER

The Essential Guide to
Competition and Strategy

HARVARD BUSINESS REVIEW PRESS

Boston, Massachusetts

No part of this publication may be reproduced, stored in or introduced into a
retrieval system, or transmitted, in any form, or by any means (electronic,
mechanical, photocopying, recording, or otherwise), without the prior
permission of the publisher. Requests for permission should be directed to
permissions@hbsp.harvard.edu, or mailed to Permissions, Harvard Business
School Publishing, 60 Harvard Way, Boston, Massachusetts 02163.

Library of Congress Cataloging-in-Publication Data

Magretta, Joan, 1948–
    Understanding Michael Porter : the essential guide to competition and
strategy / Joan Magretta.
        p. cm.
    Includes bibliographical references.
    ISBN 978-1-4221-6059-6 (alk. paper)
    1. Porter, Michael E., 1947–   2. Competition.   3. Strategic planning.
4. Management.   I. Title.
    HD41.P6776 2012
    658.4'012—dc23

                                                    2011022624

The paper used in this publication meets the requirements of the American
National Standard for Permanence of Paper for Publications and Documents in
Libraries and Archives Z39.48-1992.

By his example, Arthur Rosin, my uncle, taught me the pleasures of understanding and explaining. This book is dedicated to him, to Betty Rosin, and to my parents, Cyrille and Eugene Gorin.

Contents

Acknowledgments

The Michael Porter I know is first and foremost a gifted teacher. If this book succeeds in helping readers understand Porter's ideas in their full richness, it is thanks in large measure to his encouragement, his guidance, and his patience in explaining those ideas to me. As this book progressed, he carefully reviewed every chapter, giving generously both his time and his laser-sharp attention.

The company examples I have used to illustrate Porter's ideas draw not only on his work, but also on that of many researchers and business writers. Where I have used published sources, I cite them in the chapter notes. I also want to acknowledge the unpublished work done by the fine research associates at the Institute for Strategy and Competitiveness (ISC) at Harvard Business School (HBS), and especially by Andrew Funderburk.

Many colleagues and friends made helpful suggestions about earlier drafts of this book. Three of them went far beyond the call of duty. Jan Rivkin, who teaches strategy at HBS, did his best to keep me from cutting too many intellectual corners. Ellyn McColgan, a seasoned executive, was relentless in asking how Porter's work matters to managers. Paula Duffy, the distinguished publisher and book lover extraordinaire, provided invaluable advice about every aspect of this project. In addition I am grateful for the suggestions of Regina Fazio Maruca and Alice Howard; and for the support of Chris Allen, of Baker Library; Lydia Graham, of the ISC; and Allison Peter of Harvard Business Review Press.

We all need wise counselors and cheerleaders. Rafe Sagalyn and Cyrille Gorin were mine, urging me to write this book in the first place and helping me to get started. Melinda Merino has been the consummate editor. Her judgment and support have made this a better book.

Lastly, special thanks go to my husband, Bill Magretta. This isn't the obligatory spousal thank-you-for-putting-up-with-me. Bill is, and always has been, my secret weapon, the smartest reader I know.

Introduction

MICHAEL PORTER DIDN'T GET to be a giant in the field of competition and strategy by hunting small game. Very early in his career, he went after the single biggest and most consequential question in business: Why are some companies more profitable than others? One big question led to another. Why are some industries consistently more profitable than others, and what does this mean for the manager developing a strategy? Why are some countries or regions more successful than others, and what does this mean for companies in a global era? Since the publication of his groundbreaking classics, *Competitive Strategy* (1980) and *Competitive Advantage* (1985), Michael Porter has been steadily building answers to these fundamental questions about competition and competitive success. What could be more important for managers?

The thing about classics, as Mark Twain once observed, is that they are often books "that everybody wants to have read and nobody wants to read." Tackling Porter's work can be a bit like undertaking a serious exercise regimen. It will be good for you, even transformative. But it won't be easy, especially for managers who already have too much on their plates. Where to begin? How to navigate thousands of pages of writing, some of it written for scholars as well as managers?

Do you start with the earliest work, which is also the densest? Or do you try to jump in on the latest thinking, without first mastering the basics? The good news is that Porter's work is ambitious and deep. That is the bad news as well: his writing demands more effort and concentration than many readers today think they can spare.

But if you are serious about strategy, Porter's work is the foundation. This book distills the essence of that work for managers. If there can be such a thing as a book-length executive summary, this is it. My premise in writing this book is very simply that clear strategic thinking is essential for any manager in any setting, and Porter's work lays out the basic principles and frameworks you need to master. My goal is to present the essential Porter in a form that can be more easily digested and put to work than the original. But, to extend my metaphor, if you really want to digest these critically important ideas, you have to be willing to chew on them before you swallow. Strategy is not fast food, and neither is Porter.

"The essence of strategy," Porter often says, "is choosing what not to do." You might want to read that last sentence a second time, because it probably accounts for more failures of strategy than any other cause. In setting out my strategy for this book, I resolve to practice what Porter preaches. In a nutshell, here is what this book is *not*:

- It is not an academic book for scholars of strategy. This book is aimed at managers, and at those who advise and work with them.

- It is not an attempt to summarize *all* of Porter's work. This book focuses on competition and strategy, leaving out lots of great work on topics such as economic development or the application of competitive principles to social problems such as health care and the environment.

- It is not an extension of Porter's work. I do, however, integrate ideas that were developed at different stages in Porter's career, updating the earlier work to reflect later extensions of it. I have benefited from Porter's full cooperation, including access to the latest material from unpublished speech transcripts and lectures.

- It is not primarily a how-to book, in the sense that a book about aerodynamics and the principles of flight would not, alone, qualify you for a pilot's license. This is more of a "how-to-think-about" book, one that will help you to recognize a good (or bad) strategy when you see one and to tell the difference between a solid strategy and the latest management fad.

Why Now?

Porter's work, while never trendy and always relevant, has never been as timely for so many people working in both the private and the public sectors as it is today. This is a time of enormous economic upheaval in many industries and countries around the world. Amidst that upheaval, competition is at a crossroads. It is extolled by some as a path, indeed the *only* path, to growth and prosperity. It is feared and hated by others who see it as a destructive race to the bottom. And strategy itself has come under fire: some argue that execution, not strategy, is the only path to competitive success. They claim that even if an organization creates a competitive advantage, it simply cannot last in today's hypercompetitive world, so why bother? These are dangerous misconceptions. Master the essential Porter and you will understand not only how companies sustain competitive advantages for decades, but also why strategy is even more important—not less so—in turbulent and uncertain times.

Unfortunately, too many managers get their Porter second hand, and what they usually end up getting is both inadequate and inaccurate. I'll try to fix that by laying out Porter's ideas as concisely as possible without dumbing them down. Along the way, I'll highlight the most common misconceptions about strategy and Porter's work.

Why Me?

I first encountered Michael Porter's work when I was an MBA student at Harvard in the early 1980s and his course, "Industry and Competitive Analysis," was the hottest new offering in the curriculum. This was the course that launched a thousand strategy consultants, and I was one of them. At Bain & Company, the firm where I eventually became a partner, Porter's books didn't just sit on everyone's shelf. They were read, annotated, reread, and applied.

Over the course of my career, I've worked with clients in industries ranging from biotech and big pharma to fashion apparel to heavy manufacturing, and with nonprofits in a variety of fields. No matter the industry or the company, for-profit or not, I have always found Porter's work to be essential in making sense of what was going on. Why is this company, in this market space, thriving or flailing? Why is that organization stuck in a kind of satisfactory underperformance? It could do better; it should do better. What's wrong? Much of the good strategy work I've seen over three decades builds—consciously or not—on the foundation that Porter created.

By the early 1990s I had become the strategy editor at *Harvard Business Review* (HBR), where Porter is a leading author. He had often worked with editors who had academic or publishing backgrounds; my first-hand business experience added another dimension. I knew the theory and, as the HBR strategy editor, engaged with the brightest lights in the field. But I also understood the challenges managers face in the real world and brought that perspective to our many projects.

Those included some of Porter's most influential articles for HBR. Two are especially relevant for this book: "What Is Strategy?" (1996), one of the most-cited and best-selling HBR articles of all time, and "The Five Competitive Forces That Shape Strategy" (2008), a major update of the classic that put Porter on the map. I have also assisted Porter on many articles, books, op ed pieces, and presentations as he tackled a wide range of current topics—competition in health care, environmental sustainability, the business potential of inner cities, the local versus global dynamic in competition, the success and failure of Japanese companies, the role of leadership in strategy.

My collaboration with Porter continued after I left HBR to write a book of my own on the general manager's often-impossible job (*What Management Is: How It Works and Why It's Everyone's Business*). Porter then invited me to join his Harvard Business School–based Institute for Strategy and Competitiveness (ISC) as a senior associate, an affiliation that continues the working relationship begun almost two decades ago. Full disclosure: I am not an employee, nor do I depend on Porter for any substantial financial support. My enormous respect for his work rests purely on its merits.

The Big Leap

As readers of business books well know, management gurus come and go with alarming frequency. Why, then, does Porter's work endure? What makes this work so different and so important? Porter's is the rare intellect that successfully bridges the divide between economic theory and business practice. In the oft-told joke, one economist says to another, "Sure, it works in reality. But will it work in theory?" Porter's work endures—and is so widely cited and used—because it works in both realms, theory and practice.

Bridging the divide is an apt metaphor for Porter's career. Picture this scene. The Harvard Business School (HBS) sits majestically along the banks of the Charles River, on the Boston side. Harvard University's vaunted economics department is housed "across the river," on the more traditionally intellectual Cambridge side. Crossing the river takes just a few minutes by footbridge. But as a young graduate student in the early 1970s, first earning an MBA on one side of the river and then a PhD on the other, Michael Porter confronted a seemingly impassable intellectual divide. To put it bluntly, neither side had much use for the other.

Looking back, here's how he describes it: "The HBS research tradition saw the enterprise as an incredible complex entity. Thousands of things mattered. Every situation is unique, because it consists of different individuals, different markets, different products. Therefore, the way to study management was through in-depth cases and field research . . . . The economics tradition is completely different. In economics, you model a phenomenon. That model . . . does not try to replicate the phenomenon or capture it fully. Economic models abstract the essence of the phenomenon and represent it mathematically."

Trained in both "schools," Porter felt that neither one adequately explained what happens in competition. Case studies captured the complexities of an individual situation, but in so doing, failed to see the forest for the trees. There was no way to generalize. No framework for looking at industries. No way to think comprehensively about costs. Economic modeling went too far in the other direction. Because formal models could capture only those aspects of competition that could be solved mathematically, they reduced the richness and multidimensionality of competition to an abstraction that was too far removed from reality to be useful. For example, economists' models "simplified" competition by assuming that every firm was more or less the same. Not a very helpful assumption for managers!

Porter took a different path, creating what he calls "frameworks." In his own words, "My frameworks provide a set of logical relationships that are really fundamental. They're like physics—if you're going to have higher profitability, you've got to have a higher price or a lower cost. That industry competition is driven by the five forces. That the firm is a collection of activities. These frameworks provide basic, fundamental, and I believe unchangeable relationships about the 'matter' of competition."

Porter drew on what each side of the river did best. He did the kind of data-intensive, analytic work that tested and extended the concepts of a field of economics called industrial organization (IO). He also pored through literally hundreds of cases, looking to extract the defining elements of competition that would apply across all industries. As Porter explains it, these elements had to be intuitive to managers. That is, if you present one of the frameworks to a manager, it will "make sense" in the context of his or her industry.

Porter's frameworks initially faced criticism on both sides of the river, but especially from Business School colleagues who complained that they were "too abstract." Hard as it is to imagine today, his career prospects there seemed uncertain. The first of Porter's frameworks, the five forces, now taught in every serious business program around the world, was a big leap. And, as Porter remembers, "It was a very uncomfortable leap."

But it was crucial. In a field where so-called gurus and their best sellers come and go, Porter's work has rightly stood the test of time. Managers are regularly bombarded with "groundbreaking ideas" that purport to explain everything but which, in fact, are typically relevant only to some more limited phenomenon of the moment. At best, these are tools with a useful, but short, half-life. At worst, they are fads that send managers down destructive paths.

In contrast, Porter has steadfastly focused on timeless principles. His is the general theory that applies in all cases. If you enter Porter's world, you will have to do without the catchy metaphors: no blue oceans, no dancing elephants, no moving cheeses. What you will get, instead, is a rigorous and clear mapping between your strategy and your organization's financial performance, or, in the case of nonprofit organizations, between your strategy and your effectiveness in meeting a given social goal.

Porter occupies a unique position. Among academics, he is the most cited scholar in economics and business. At the same time, his ideas are the most widely used in practice by business and government leaders around the world. His frameworks have become the foundation of the strategy field.

A Chapter-by-Chapter Road Map

I offer this chapter-by-chapter road map to prepare you for what lies ahead. This book is divided into two parts: the first deals with competition, the second with strategy.

Part 1: What Is Competition?

I start with competition in Part 1 for the simple reason that if there were no competition, there would be no need for strategy. Competitive rivalry is a relentless process working against a company's ability to find and maintain an advantage. In Part 1, we'll do the important prep work for strategy, spelling out how competition works and dispelling the most popular, and misleading, misconceptions about competition and competitive advantage.

- **Chapter 1. Competition: The Right Mind-Set.** Misconceptions of what competition is and how it works give rise to mistakes in strategy. The most common error of all is that competitive success comes from "being the best." This mindset is highly intuitive. It is also self-destructive, leading to a zero-sum race to the bottom. Only by competing to be unique can an organization achieve sustained, superior performance.

- **Chapter 2. The Five Forces: Competing for Profits.** We'll see that competition is much more than a direct contest between rivals over who gets the sale. It's a broader struggle over profits, a tug-of-war over who will capture the value an industry creates. Porter's best-known framework, the five forces, helps you visualize the competition for profits at work in every industry. Any assessment of your competitive arena must start here. Using the five forces to declare an industry attractive or unattractive isn't the point, although that's a common misperception. Instead, use the framework to gain insight about your industry's performance and your own.

- **Chapter 3. Competitive Advantage: The Value Chain and Your P&L.** Managers use the term *competitive advantage* so loosely that it has come to mean almost anything an organization thinks it is good at. Porter's definition is more rigorously grounded in economic fundamentals. Properly understood, competitive advantage allows you to follow the precise link between the value you create, how you create it (your value chain), and how you perform (your P&L). Competitive advantage is commonly understood as the weapon you use to trounce rivals. For Porter, it's fundamentally about creating value, and about doing so differently from rivals. In this way, competitive advantage is about how your value chain will be different and your P&L better than the industry average.

Part 2: What Is Strategy?

Part 2 answers the question, *what is strategy?* You can call any plan or program a strategy, and that's how most people use the word. But a *good* strategy, one that will result in superior economic performance, is something else. Broadly speaking, strategy is the antidote to competition. Specifically, a robust strategy is defined by its ability to pass five basic tests.

- **Chapter 4. Creating Value: The Core.** What does it mean to stake out a distinctive competitive position? The obvious answer lies in the unique value proposition a company offers its customers. This, in fact, is the first test of strategy. But Porter's second test is neither obvious nor intuitive. A distinctive value proposition will translate into a meaningful strategy only if the best set of activities to deliver it is different from the activities performed by rivals. Competitive advantage lies in the activities, in choosing to perform activities differently or to perform different activities from rivals. A tailored value chain is strategy's second test.

- **Chapter 5. Trade-offs: The Linchpin.** The third test of strategy may well be the hardest. Making trade-offs means accepting limits—saying no to some customers, for example, so that you can better serve others. Trade-offs arise when choices are incompatible. Because a successful strategy will attract imitators, choices that are difficult to copy are essential. Some people, in fact, argue that competitive advantages can no longer be sustained. Trade-offs explain why that's not true. Trade-offs are the economic linchpins of strategy for two reasons. First, they are an important source of differences in prices and costs among rivals. Second, they make it difficult for rivals to copy what you do without compromising their own strategies.

- **Chapter 6. Fit: The Amplifier.** The fourth test of strategy is fit. Fit has to do with how the activities in the value chain relate to one another. At one level, the idea of fit is completely intuitive. Every general manager knows the importance—and the difficulty—of aligning the various functional areas needed to compete in a business. But fit goes beyond simple alignment to amplify a competitive advantage and to make it more sustainable. Its role in strategy highlights yet another popular misconception: that competitive success can be explained by one *core competence*, the *one* thing you do really well. Good strategies depend on the connection among *many* things, on making *interdependent* choices. A common piece of advice for managers has been to focus on their core activities and to outsource the rest. Fit challenges that bit of conventional wisdom.

- **Chapter 7. Continuity: The Enabler.** Competition is dynamic. Everyone can name once-proud companies brought low by their failure to change. But continuity, as pedestrian as it sounds, is also essential. Although the spotlight is more often directed at companies that change too little, Porter's fifth test is about an equal, if not greater, mistake: companies can change too much, and in the wrong ways. It takes time to develop real competitive advantage, to understand the value you create, to achieve tailoring, trade-offs, and fit. If you grasp the role of continuity in strategy, it will change your thinking about change itself. Paradoxically, continuity of strategy improves an organization's ability to adapt and to innovate.

- Epilogue: A Short List of Implications. I offer up a highly distilled list of takeaways as a way both of summarizing where we have been and how Porter's core ideas can be applied in practice.

Beyond the body of the book, you'll find more than the usual end matter:

- FAQs: An Interview with Michael Porter. This is a must-read interview with Michael Porter in which he answers the questions about competition and strategy managers most often ask him. Among them are the following: What are the greatest obstacles to strategy and the most common mistakes companies make? How can you grow without undermining your strategy? How should you think about disruption and new business models?

- A Porter Glossary: Key Concepts. This contains user-friendly descriptions of key concepts along with suggestions for further reading for those who want to go beyond the essentials covered in this volume.

A Cautionary Note About Case Examples

In presenting Porter's frameworks, I make extensive use of business case examples. They are a double-edged sword. They make ideas come to life by showing them in action, in flesh-and-blood organizations. But like flesh and blood, they can age quickly. No sooner has the book rolled off the press or been downloaded than events begin to overtake the example. As I was writing about one company's competitive dilemma, for example, it declared bankruptcy. That story remains in the book, since it underscores my point. But for the record, my objective is to convey timeless principles, ideas that don't change even if the facts of the case do. Competition is demanding. Even outstanding companies make mistakes. Good strategies can be enduring, but none last forever.

Then there is the question of which facts to present. Porter reviewed successive drafts of this book, and he kept pushing me for "more numbers." But this is not a textbook. For readers who want more of an analytic workout, I'll suggest some great resources. Nevertheless, Porter's point, an important one, is that strategy requires clear, analytic thinking. It's not rocket science, but it's not for the fuzzy-minded. Quantifying forces you to be precise. That said, the "overtaken by events" argument is especially relevant when it comes to data about companies and markets. I ended up with enough numbers, I hope, to make Porter's point without getting bogged down. Where I have used precise numbers to reflect, for example, a company's relative cost advantage or the number of customers it serves, I can almost guarantee that by the time you read this, the data will have changed. Why, then, present numbers that are probably inaccurate? To make the point that strategy is—or should be—fact based. Amen to that.

PART ONE

What Is Competition?

S TRATEGY EXPLAINS how an organization, faced with competition, will achieve superior performance. But what exactly is competition? How does it work? What do managers need to understand about the nature of competition and competitive success? What's the right definition of superior performance? This section lays out the basics.

First, the right mind-set. Managers often think about competition as a form of warfare, a zero-sum battle for dominance in which only the alphas prevail. This, we'll see in chapter 1, is a deeply flawed and destructive way of thinking. The key to competitive success—for businesses and nonprofits alike—lies in an organization's ability to create unique value. Porter's prescription: aim to be unique, not best. Creating value, not beating rivals, is at the heart of competition.

Second, the right analytics. Where does superior performance come from? Porter's answer can be divided into two parts. The first part is attributable to *the structure of the industry* in which competition takes place. This is the subject of chapter 2. Porter starts with the industry because competing to be unique is a choice made against a specific and relevant set of rivals, and because the structure of the industry determines how the value it creates is shared. Porter's five forces framework explains industry structure and the profitability any company can expect simply by being "average."

The second part is attributable to *the company's relative position* within its industry. Strategic positioning reflects choices a company makes about the kind of value it will create and how that value will be created. Here, competitive advantage and the value chain are the relevant frameworks. In chapter 3 we'll trace the links between a company's competitive position, its value chain, and its P&L.

These core frameworks set the stage for strategy: they explain why there are large and sustained differences in profitability *across* industries and why some companies are able to outperform others *within* an industry. This grounding in the economic fundamentals of competition provides the foundation for strategy.

CHAPTER 1

Competition:

The Right Mind-Set

STRATEGY IS ONE OF the most dangerous concepts in business. Why dangerous? Because while most managers agree that it is terrifically important, once you start paying attention to how the word is used you will soon be wondering whether it means anything at all. Fans of GE's legendary CEO Jack Welch say their strategy is to be number 1 or number 2 in their business (or else!). For the new CEO of a *Fortune* 100 company, the strategy is "to grow." For an energy company executive, the strategy is to "make key acquisitions." A software developer says, "Our strategy is our people." The strategy of a leading nonprofit is to "double the number of people we serve." And then there is Google's famous "Don't be evil." Is that a strategy?

By the time you reach the end of this book, you will appreciate why *none* of the above would qualify as a "strategy," which for Porter is shorthand for "a *good* competitive strategy that will result in *sustainably superior performance*." None of the above formulations tells you what will enable the organization in question to outperform the competition. Some tell you what their goal or aspiration is; others highlight key actions; some single out values. But none of them really tackles the core question, *performance in the face of competition*. What value will your organization create? And how will you capture some of that value for yourself? That, Michael Porter tells us, is strategy's job.

Strategy explains how an organization, faced with competition, will achieve superior performance. The definition is deceptively simple in part because the words are so familiar that we rarely stop to think about what they mean. But if you do, you will quickly realize that these terms are loaded. What is competition? How does it work? How do organizations "win"? What, exactly, does *superior performance* mean?

Strategy explains how an organization, faced with competition, will achieve superior performance. The definition is deceptively simple.

Most managers worry about competition. They know that it's pervasive. They have an uncomfortable sense that it is breathing down their necks. They know that in order to survive they must deal with it. And in order to thrive, they have to find a "competitive advantage," a term rarely used before Porter made it popular. And yet, Porter tells us, one of the reasons so many companies fail to develop good strategies is that the people running them operate with fundamental misconceptions about what competition is and how it works. This is critical because if there were no competition, there would be no need for strategy, no need to come up with a way to "win," to outperform your rivals. But, of course, competition is everywhere, even in so-called market "spaces" served primarily by nonprofit organizations.

How you think about competition will define the choices you make about how you are going to compete. It will impact your ability to assess those choices critically. That is why before we can even begin to talk about strategy, we need to tackle the question of competition and competitive advantage.

Why Not the Best?

Interviewed on the day the "new" General Motors went public in 2010, CEO Dan Akerson said his company, now free of its legacy costs, was ready to compete. "May the best car win!" he told reporters. How often have you heard an organization's leaders urging their people to be "the best"? How often have you heard the call to make your company the "best in its industry"? Companies proudly proclaim that they produce the "best" products, provide the "best" service, and attract the "best" talent. These phrases reflect an underlying belief about the nature of competition that feels so intuitively correct to most people that it is almost never examined or questioned. If you want to win, it's obvious that you should be the best. Or is it?

Michael Porter has a name for this syndrome. He calls it *competition to be the best*. It is, he will tell you, absolutely the wrong way to think about competition. If you start out with this flawed idea of how competition works, it will lead you inevitably to a flawed strategy. And that will lead to mediocre performance.

For most managers, vying to be the best is what competition is all about. This belief is reinforced by popular metaphors drawn from warfare and sports. Management writers—and leaders trying to inspire people—are drawn to these metaphors because they are vivid and engaging. They lend emotion, drama, and consequence to business competition. But metaphors can be misleading. Although they highlight how one thing has *elements* that are *like* another, they never mean that one thing is *identical* to another.

In war, there can be only one winner. Victory requires that the enemy be crippled or destroyed. In business, however, you can win without annihilating your rivals. For decades, Walmart has been a winner in discount retailing, for example, but so has Target. Each offers a different and distinctive mix of merchandise, aimed at meeting different customer needs. Walmart is the workhorse of discounters, offering "everyday low prices." Target is more of a show horse, appealing to customers who want flair along with low prices. In business, multiple winners can thrive and coexist. Competition focuses more on meeting customer needs than on demolishing rivals. Just look around. Because there are so many needs to serve, there are many ways to win.

The sports analogy is just as misleading. Athletes vie with each other to see who will be crowned "the best." They focus on outperforming their rivals. They compete to win. But in sports, there is one contest with one set of rules. There can be only one winner. Business competition is more complex, more open ended and multidimensional. Within an industry, there can be multiple contests, not just one, based on which customers and needs are to be served. McDonald's is a winner in fast food, specifically fast burgers. But In-N-Out Burger thrives on slow burgers. Its customers are happy to wait ten minutes or more (an eternity by McDonald's stopwatch) to get nonprocessed, fresh burgers cooked to order on homemade buns. Rather than enter a particular race with a particular rival, as Porter would put it, companies can choose to create their own event.

It's always hard to break a mental habit, but harder still if you are unaware that you have one in the first place. That's the problem with the *competition-to-be-the-best* mind-set. It is typically a tacit way of thinking, not an explicit model. The nature of competition is simply taken for granted. But, says Porter, it shouldn't be. In the vast majority of businesses, there is simply no such thing as "the best." Think about it for a moment. Is there a best car? A best hamburger? A best mobile phone?

In the vast majority of businesses, there is simply no such thing as "the best."

Consider a business as prosaic as seating for airport waiting areas. You would think that there would be a "best" here—standardized seating that is functional and durable. Well, you would be wrong. Different airports have different needs. Some want waiting passengers to shop. They don't want seats that are too comfortable. Some need the flexibility to reconfigure waiting areas. They don't want long rows of fixed seats. Many airports have to watch their spending. For others, however, money is no object. Airports in the Middle East, for example, have been big buyers of luxury designs. Some airports, those that handle a steady flow of deported refugees, for example, value seats built to take extraordinary abuse. London-based OMK makes "prison-worthy" seating, the industry's highest standard, using self-sealing polyurethane that can withstand a stabbing without showing the knife scar. So much for the idea that there is one "best" airport seat.

Now think about all of the industries in the economy. In how many does the idea of "being the best" make real sense? In most industries, there are many different customers with different needs. The best hotel for one customer is not the best for another. The best sales encounter for one customer is not the best for another. There is no best art museum, no one best way to promote environmental sustainability.

Nor is there such a thing as an absolute best when it comes to performing functions such as production or logistics or marketing. For a nonprofit organization, there is no best way to do fundraising or attract volunteers. The best always depends on what you are trying to accomplish. Thus, the first flaw of *competition to be the best* is that if an organization sets out to be the best, it sets itself an impossible goal.

But that's not all. If rivals all pursue the "one best way" to compete, they will find themselves on a collision course. Everyone in the industry will listen to the same advice and follow the same prescription. Companies will benchmark each other's practices and products (see "One-Upmanship Is Not Strategy"). Competing to be the best leads inevitably to a destructive, zero-sum competition that no one can win. As offerings converge, gain for one becomes loss for the other. This is the very essence of "zero sum." I win only if you lose.

If rivals all pursue the "one best way" to compete, they will find themselves on a collision course.

The airline industry has suffered from this sort of competition for decades. If American Airlines tries to win new customers by offering free meals on its New York to Miami route, then Delta will be forced to match it—leaving both companies worse off. Both will have incurred added costs, but neither will be able to charge more, and neither will end up with more seats filled. Every time one company makes a move, its rivals will jump to match it. With everyone chasing after the same customer, there will be a contest over every sale.

This, says Porter, is *competitive convergence*. Over time, rivals begin to look alike as one difference after another erodes. Customers

One-Upmanship Is Not Strategy

The first salvo in what came to be known as the Hotel Bed Wars was fired in 1999. After a year of testing mattresses, pillows, and bed linens and investing tens of millions of dollars in the effort, Westin Hotels and Resorts introduced the industry's first branded bed, its custom-designed Heavenly Bed. "We wanted to differentiate ourselves from the competition," a Westin executive explained.

As you might expect, rivals didn't take long to respond, piling on the pillows and swaddling guests in ever-higher thread counts: Hilton with its Serenity Bed, Marriott with its Revive Collection, Hyatt with its Hyatt Grant Bed, Radisson with its Sleep Number Bed, and Crowne Plaza with its Sleep Advantage Program.

By 2006, the press declared that the Bed Wars had come to an end, but not before every major rival had made large investments developing, installing, and promoting its own branded offering. Guests at every hotel in the category can now rest assured that "bed quality" will not differentiate one hotel from another. As is often the case, one company's attempt to be "the best" ended up raising the bar for everyone. It's not surprising, with this approach to competing, that long-term profitability in the hotel industry has been chronically low, a topic we'll explore more rigorously in chapter 2.

Reports are mixed about whether, in this case, the industry was able to raise prices enough to benefit from its investment in upgraded bedding. If not, customers captured the value of this spending. But even if this particular move benefited the industry overall, when all rivals compete on the same dimension, no one gains a competitive advantage.

26 of26

Be Number 1 or Number 2

Either be number 1 or number 2 in your industry, or get out. That ultimatum was made famous by former GE CEO Jack Welch, but it is just one version of what is arguably the most influential form of competition to be the best. Another name for the same idea is "winner takes all." This model holds that companies win by getting bigger and, ultimately, by dominating their industries. If size drives competitive success, then growth is essential to achieving market share and volume. Companies pursue economies of scale and scope in the belief that these will be decisive in determining competitive advantage and profitability.

Of course there is at least a grain of truth in this thinking, which is precisely what makes it so dangerous. There are economies of scale and advantages to being bigger in most businesses. This was certainly the case in some of GE's scale-intensive businesses during the Welch era. But before you assume that bigger is always better, it is critical to run the numbers for *your* business. Too often the goal is chosen because it sounds good, whether or not the economics of the business support the logic. In industry after industry, Porter notes that economies of scale are exhausted at a relatively small share of industry sales. There is no systematic evidence that indicates that industry leaders are the most profitable or successful firms. To cite one notorious example, General Motors was the world's largest car

are left with nothing but price as the basis for their choices. This has happened in airlines, in many categories of consumer electronics, and in personal computers, with the notable exception of Apple, the one major company in that industry that has consistently marched to its own drummer.

company for a period of decades, a fact that didn't prevent its descent into bankruptcy. To the extent that size mattered at all, it might be more accurate to say that GM was too big to succeed. Meanwhile, BMW, small by industry standards, has a history of superior returns. Over the past decade (2000–2009), its average return on invested capital was 50 percent higher than the industry average.

Companies only have to be "big enough," which rarely means they have to dominate. Often "big enough" is just 10 percent of the market. Yet companies under the influence of winner-takes-all thinking tend to pursue illusory scale advantages. In doing so, they are likely to damage their own performance by cutting price to gain volume, by overextending themselves to serve all market segments, and by pursuing overpriced mergers and acquisitions. The auto industry over the past couple of decades has exhibited all of the above tendencies, to disastrous effect.

The winner-takes-all model presupposes incorrectly that there is one scale curve in an industry and that all companies must move down that curve.* That is, it assumes that all rivals are competing to offer the universally best product or service. In practice, most industries exhibit multiple scale curves, each based on serving different needs.

*A scale curve shows the costs of production as a function of the total quantity produced. A downward-sloping cost curve means the company with the biggest volume will have the lowest unit costs.

This inevitable descent into price competition is the business equivalent of mutually assured destruction. And it's not just the producers who suffer. Customers, suppliers, and employees often become collateral damage as rivals are squeezed for resources and forced to cut costs. When all else fails and pressure on prices has destroyed an industry's profitability, often the remedy is to limit competition through consolidation. Companies swallow each other up, thus reducing the number of rivals and allowing one or a few companies to dominate the market.

But Isn't "The Best" Good for Customers?

In what classical economic theory calls "perfect competition," evenly matched rivals selling equivalent products go head to head, driving prices (and profits) down. This, for Porter, is the essence of competition to be the best. According to classical theory, perfect competition is the most efficient way to promote social welfare. The lesson taught in Econ 101 is that what's good for customers (lower prices) is bad for companies (lower profits), and vice versa.

But Porter offers a more nuanced and complex view of what actually happens when companies compete to be the best. Customers may benefit from lower prices as rivals imitate and match each other's offerings, but they may also be forced to sacrifice choice. When an industry converges around a standard offering, the "average" customer may fare well. But remember that averages are made up of some customers who want more and some who want less. There will be individuals in both groups who will not be well served by the average.

The needs of some customers may be overserved by what the industry offers. In plain English, you will pay more for features you don't need. As I write this, it's hard not to think about my word processing software. It is also true of most of the appliances in my kitchen. These products have become unnecessarily complex and feature-laden for my needs, and I am both a professional writer and an accomplished cook. As they have become more complex, they have also become more prone to costly failures.

The needs of other customers may be underserved. Think about the last flight you took. It probably met the basic need of getting you where you needed to be. But was it a pleasant experience? Are you eager to fly again?

When choice is limited, value is often destroyed. As a customer, you are either paying too much for extras you don't want, or you are forced to make do with what's offered, even if it's not really what you need.

For companies, the picture isn't any brighter. With all companies heading for the same place, it is difficult to stay in the lead for long. Competitive advantage will be temporary. Companies work hard, but their gains in quality and cost are not rewarded with attractive profitability. In turn, chronically poor profitability undermines investment in the future, making it harder to improve value for customers or fend off rivals.

In practice, then, head-to-head competition is rarely "perfect" for either customers or the companies that serve them. Yet Porter notes with some alarm that it is precisely this kind of zero-sum competition that has come increasingly to dominate management thinking.

Competition to Be Unique

For Porter, strategic competition means choosing a path different from that of others. Instead of competing to be the best, companies can—and should—*compete to be unique*. This concept is all about value. It's about uniqueness in the value you create and how you create it. Before 2008, for example, if you wanted to get from Madrid to Barcelona, you could take a short flight or you could spend the better part of a day in your car or on a slow train. Roughly 90 percent of the six million travelers between Madrid and Barcelona chose to fly. In 2008, high-speed train service gave travelers a new choice. Despite the fact that the train now charges more than the low-cost airlines, there has been a dramatic shift away from flying on that route.

Strategic competition means choosing a path different from that of others.

Both plane and train will get you from Madrid to Barcelona, but the train offers a different kind of value. The AVE (Alta Velocidad Española) allows you to go from city center to city center in an assigned, reclining seat with computer outlets, food, and entertainment. You can say *adios* to the hassles of contemporary air travel, the security screening, the carry-on restrictions, the inevitable delays. And for those who think green, the AVE offers another benefit: substantially lower carbon dioxide emissions than flying or driving. That cluster of differences, that uniqueness, is the very essence of competitive advantage, a topic we will explore fully in the chapters to come. Airline executives in Spain may have been defining their competition as other airlines. But customers who switch clearly don't see it that way—and value is ultimately defined by customers.

Competition to be unique reflects a different mind-set and a different way of thinking about the nature of competition. Here, companies pursue distinctive ways of competing aimed at serving different sets of needs and customers. The focus, in other words, is on creating superior value for the chosen customers, not on imitating and matching rivals. Here, because customers have real choices, price is only one competitive variable. Some competitors, such as Vanguard or IKEA, will have strategies emphasizing low price. Others, such as BMW, Apple, or Four Seasons, will command a premium price by offering different features or service levels. Customers will pay more (or less) depending on how they perceive the value that's offered to them.

Competing to be unique is unlike warfare in that one company's success does not require its rivals to fail. It is unlike competition in sports because every company can chose to invent its own game. A better analogy than war or sports might be the performing arts. There can be many good singers or actors—each outstanding and successful in a distinctive way. Each finds and creates an audience. The more good performers there are, the more audiences grow and the arts flourish. This kind of value creation is the essence of positive-sum competition.

While zero-sum competition is rightly depicted as a race to the bottom, positive-sum competition produces better outcomes. To be sure, not every company will succeed. Competition will weed out the underperformers. But companies that do a good job can earn sustainable returns because they create more value; nonprofit organizations can do more good because they meet needs more effectively and efficiently. And customers can get real choice in how their needs are met. Competing to be the best feeds on imitation. Competing to be unique thrives on innovation.

Competition is a singular noun. But Porter reminds us that in practice, competition takes almost as many forms as there are industries. At one extreme is competition to be the best. At the other is its polar opposite, competition to be unique. One popular management book, *Blue Ocean Strategy*, uses the metaphor of red oceans versus blue to distinguish bloody head-to-head competition from the clear blue seas where, its authors say, competition is irrelevant. This is a double misconception worth highlighting. First, it mistakenly portrays Porter as a champion of bloody "red ocean strategy," when, in fact, his work stresses the opposite. Second, competition, properly understood, is never irrelevant. Most industries exist somewhere between the two extremes Porter describes, exhibiting elements of both in varying degrees. Actual practice is always messier than the frameworks that help us to see important patterns.

FIGURE 1-1

The right mind-set for competition

BE THE BEST	BE UNIQUE
Be number 1	Earn higher returns
Focus on market share	Focus on profits
Serve "best" customer with "best" product	Meet diverse needs of target customers
Compete by imitation	Compete by innovation
ZERO SUM **A race that no one** **can win**	**POSITIVE SUM** **Multiple winners,** **many events**

But Porter's distinction between these two radically different approaches to competition, summed up in figure 1-1, raises a critical point for managers. There is nothing foreordained or predetermined about the path that industries take to zero-sum or to positive-sum competition. There is nothing inherent in the industry—whether it is high tech or low, whether it is service or manufacturing—that will determine its fate. Some industries do face tougher economic challenges than others, but the path that industries take is also the result of choices—strategic choices—that managers make about how to compete. Bad choices unleash a race to the bottom. Good choices promote healthy competition, innovation, and growth.

Competition to be unique, Porter's work teaches, can make life better across almost all fields of human endeavor—but only if managers understand that their choices will influence the kind of competition that prevails in their industry. These are choices with enormously high stakes.

Given the complexity of the manager's job, it is hardly surprising that so many hunger for simplification—a single recipe for success. It's the fast food of business thinking. But beware of anyone who claims there is only one way to win. If there were only one best way to compete, Porter reasons, many, if not all, companies would adopt it. Competition would end in stalemate at best or mutual destruction at worst. Instead, competition is multidimensional, and strategy is about making choices along *many* dimensions, not just *one*. No single prescription about which choices to make is valid for every company in every industry.

Fortunately, however, this does not mean that strategy is an intellectual free-for-all. On the contrary, there are underlying principles that can be used to analyze any competitive situation and to determine which choices make sense. Those universal economic principles are the subject of our next two chapters, as we dig deeper into the roots of superior performance.

Why are some companies more profitable than others? That's the big question we'll be working on. The answer has two parts. First, companies benefit from (or are hurt by) the structure of their industry. Second, a company's relative position within its industry can account for even more of the difference. Chapters 2 and 3 follow that two-part logic. Understanding the role of industry structure in competition is the topic of our next chapter.

CHAPTER 2

The Five Forces:

Competing for Profits

I N THE LAST CHAPTER we covered one of the most widespread misconceptions about competition: the idea that success comes from "being the best." Here we'll tackle another big misconception. Most people think of competition as a direct contest between rivals. That's the standard definition you'll find if you look it up. Apple wants to sell you an iPhone. Research In Motion promotes its device, the BlackBerry. These two rivals engage in a contest to win your smartphone business. Similarly, Yamaha competes with Steinway to sell you a piano. BMW and Audi compete to sell you a car, and Hyatt and Westin to rent you a hotel room.

But this way of thinking about competition is too narrow. The real point of competition is not to beat your rivals. It's not about winning a sale. The point is to earn profits. Competing for profits is more complex. It's a struggle involving multiple players, not just rivals, over who will capture the value an industry creates. It's true, of course, that companies compete for profits with their rivals. But they are also engaged in a struggle for profits with their customers, who would always be happier to pay less and get more. They compete with their suppliers, who would always be happier to be paid more and deliver less. They compete with producers who make products that could, in a pinch, be substituted for their own. And they compete with potential rivals as well as existing ones, because even the threat of new entrants places limits on how much they can charge their customers.

The real point of competition is not to beat your rivals. It's to earn profits.

These five forces—the intensity of rivalry among existing competitors, the bargaining power of buyers (the industry's customers), the bargaining power of suppliers, the threat of substitutes, and the threat of new entrants—determine the industry's *structure*, an important concept that may sound academic but is not (figure 2-1). If you look at a building, any building—a house, a church, a warehouse—its structure immediately gives you important information about its use, about how the building "works," how it creates shelter by enclosing space. The structure is determined by elements common to all buildings: the foundation, the walls, the roof. Similarly, you get important information about an industry by looking at its structure. The particular configuration of Porter's five forces tells you immediately how the industry "works," how it creates and shares value. It explains the industry's profitability.

Porter's research findings on the links between industry structure and profitability challenge several popular misconceptions. Porter has, in fact, found:

- First, as different from one another as industries might appear on the surface, the same forces are at work under the skin.

FIGURE 2-1

Industry structure: The five forces

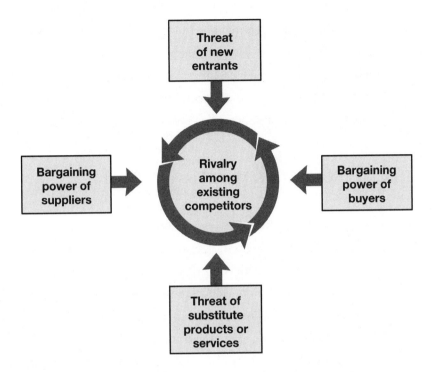

Source: From Michael E. Porter, "The Five Competitive Forces That Shape Strategy," *Harvard Business Review*, January 2008, 78–93. Copyright © 2008 by Harvard Business Publishing.

From advertising to zipper manufacturing (and every industry in between), the same five forces apply, although their relative strength and importance may differ.

- Second, industry structure determines profitability—not, as many people think, whether the industry is high growth or low, high tech or low, regulated or not, manufacturing or service. Structure trumps these other, more intuitive, categories.

- Third, industry structure is surprisingly sticky. Despite the prevailing sense that business changes with incredible rapidity, Porter discovered that industry structure—once an industry passes beyond its emerging, prestructure phase—tends to be quite stable over time. New products come and go. New technologies come and go. Things change all the time. But *structural* change—and therefore change in the average profitability of an industry—usually takes a long time.

Industry Structure: A More Powerful Tool

For any organization trying to assess or formulate strategy, the five forces framework is the place to start. Remember that strategy explains how an organization, faced with competition, will achieve superior performance. The five forces framework zeroes in on the *competition you face* and gives you the baseline for measuring *superior* performance. It explains the industry's average prices and costs, and therefore the average industry profitability you are trying to beat. Before you can make sense of your own performance (current and potential), you need insight into the industry's fundamental economics.

> The five forces framework explains the
> industry's average prices and costs, and
> therefore the average industry profitability
> you are trying to beat.

Five forces analysis answers the key question, What's going on out there in your industry? Of the many things that are happening, which ones matter for competition? What deserves your attention? Before

Porter, the prevailing framework for sizing up the environment was called SWOT, short for strengths, weaknesses, opportunities, and threats. Its intent was correct—to relate the company to its environment—but the tool was weak. If you've sat through a SWOT exercise, you know what I mean. Because there are no coherent economic principles underlying SWOT, you end up with random lists of items under each of the four headings, depending on who is in the room and what issues are top of mind that morning.

Although SWOT is still used in some quarters, it is biased (in my experience, heavily so) toward confirming managers' long-standing beliefs, whether those are based on sound economics or on an executive's personal agenda. (Consider the big acquisition that's put on the "opportunity" list because that executive once worked at the target company and now it's payback time, or maybe the deal will earn the executive a big bonus at year-end. Biases of these sorts are all too common in practice.)

Industry structure is an exponentially more powerful and objective tool for understanding the dynamics of competition. It is systematic, reducing the odds that you will miss something important. It is (or should be) built on facts and analysis, not just a listing of bullet points. Therefore it is less likely to result in a rehash of old agendas and more likely to teach you something new. It tackles the economic fundamentals of competition in a way that highlights how external forces constrain or create strategic opportunities for your company.

Assessing the Five Forces

Each of the five forces has a clear, direct, and predictable relationship to industry profitability. Here's the general rule: the more powerful the

---

The Fundamental Equation: Profit = Price − Cost

At its heart, business competition is about the struggle for profits, the tug-of-war over who gets to capture the value an industry creates. As complex and multidimensional as competition typically is, the math of profitability is simple. Porter reminds us to stay focused on the ultimate goal—profit—and on its two components, price and cost:

Unit Profit Margin = Price − Cost

Costs include *all* of the resources used in competing, including the cost of capital. These are the resources that the industry transforms to create value. Prices reflect how customers value the industry's offerings, what they are willing to pay as they weigh their alternatives.

Note that if an industry doesn't create much value for its customers, prices will barely cover costs. If the industry creates a lot of value, then structure becomes critical in understanding who gets to capture it. Industries can, and often do, create a lot of value for

---

force, the more pressure it will put on prices or costs or both, and therefore the less attractive the industry will be to its incumbents. (A reminder: Industry structure is always analyzed from the perspective of companies already in the industry. Because potential entrants must overcome entry barriers, this explains why an industry can be "attractive" to incumbents while at the same time not attracting new competitors.)

After describing each force, I'll indicate how you can assess its strength. The many examples I cite serve a dual purpose—they both illustrate the force and, at the same time, give you a sense of how specific companies have responded to the most relevant forces in their industry. People ask all the time, "How do companies use this

their customers or suppliers while the companies themselves earn very little for their efforts.

Within a given industry, the relative strength of the five forces and their specific configuration determine the industry's profit potential because they directly impact the industry's prices and its costs. Here's how each force works.

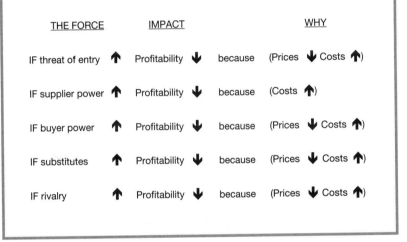

THE FORCE	IMPACT		WHY
IF threat of entry ↑	Profitability ↓	because	(Prices ↓ Costs ↑)
IF supplier power ↑	Profitability ↓	because	(Costs ↑)
IF buyer power ↑	Profitability ↓	because	(Prices ↓ Costs ↑)
IF substitutes ↑	Profitability ↓	because	(Prices ↓ Costs ↑)
IF rivalry ↑	Profitability ↓	because	(Prices ↓ Costs ↑)

framework?" By definition, any successful company has positioned itself favorably in relation to the forces that matter most in its industry. But let me stress that one of the great clarifying disciplines of Porter's approach is to force you to think clearly about your industry's structure. Start there. Then you can focus on your own and rivals' relative positions within the industry.

Buyers

If you have powerful buyers (that is, customers), they will use their clout to force prices down. They may also demand that you put more value into the product or service. In either case, industry profitability will be lower because customers will capture more of the value for themselves.

Powerful buyers will force prices down or demand more value in the product, thus capturing more of the value for themselves.

Consider the cement industry. In the United States, big, powerful construction companies account for a large percentage of the cement industry's sales. They use their clout to bargain for low prices, thus dampening the profit potential for the industry. Now let's cross the border to Mexico, where 85 percent of the cement industry's revenues come from small, individual customers. Thousands of these "ants," as they are called, are served by a handful of large producers. This imbalance in bargaining power between small, fragmented buyers and a few large sellers is a defining element of the structure of the Mexican cement industry. Market power allows the producers to charge higher prices and earn higher returns.

It's no surprise, then, that CEMEX, a leading producer in both countries, earns higher returns in Mexico, and not because it creates more value in its home market. In effect, CEMEX is competing in two distinct industries, each with its own structure. (The box "Typical Steps in Industry Analysis" later in this chapter highlights the strategic importance of defining the boundaries of a business.)

When you assess buyer power, the channels through which products are delivered can be as important as the end users. This is especially true when the channel influences the purchase decisions of the end-user customers. Investment advisors, for example, have enormous power, and the high margins that accompany that power. The emergence of powerful retailers like Home Depot and Lowe's has put enormous pressure on the makers of home improvement products.

Within an industry there may be segments of buyers with more or less negotiating power, and with greater or lesser price sensitivity. Buyers are more likely to exercise their negotiating leverage if they are price sensitive. Both industrial customers and consumers tend to be more price sensitive when what they're buying is

- Undifferentiated

- Expensive relative to their other costs or income

- Inconsequential to their own performance

A counterexample that includes all three of these conditions is the price insensitivity of makers of major motion pictures when they buy or rent production equipment. A movie camera, for example, is a highly differentiated piece of equipment. Its price is small relative to the other costs of production, but the performance of the equipment has a big impact on the success of the movie. Here quality trumps price.

Suppliers

If you have powerful suppliers, they will use their negotiating leverage to charge higher prices or to insist on more favorable terms. In either case, industry profitability will be lower because suppliers will capture more of the value for themselves. Makers of personal computers (PCs) have long struggled with the market power of both Microsoft and Intel. In Intel's case, the Intel Inside campaign effectively branded what might have otherwise become a commodity component.

> Powerful suppliers will charge higher prices
> or insist on more favorable terms, lowering
> industry profitability.

When you analyze the power of suppliers, be sure to include all of the purchased inputs that go into a product or service, including labor (i.e., your employees). The bargaining power of strong labor unions has been a perennial drag on the airline industry. Work rules such as "receipt and dispatch," for example, allowed only licensed mechanics to wave planes to or from airport gates, even though lower-paid baggage handlers or other ground crew were competent to perform this job. Repairs were done mostly at night, but this rule meant mechanics had to be scheduled 24/7, and the airlines had to hire many more of them than were needed for maintenance and repair. This rule, now gone, was effectively a job creation program for the high-paid mechanics, and a profit drain for the airline industry.

How do you assess the power of suppliers and buyers? The same set of questions applies to both, so I'll give you one list instead of two. Both suppliers and buyers tend to be powerful if:

- They are large and concentrated relative to a fragmented industry (think Goliath versus many Davids). What percentage of an industry's purchases/sales does a supplier/buyer represent? Look at the data and map out how it is trending. How painful would it be to lose that supplier or that customer? Industries with high fixed costs (e.g., telecommunications equipment and offshore drilling) are especially vulnerable to large buyers.

- The industry needs them more than they need the industry. In some cases, there may be no alternative suppliers, at least in the short term. Doctors and airline pilots, to cite two examples, have historically exercised tremendous bargaining power because their skills have been both essential and in short supply. China produces 95 percent of the world's supply of neodymium, a rare earth metal needed by Toyota and other automakers for electric motors. Neodymium prices quadrupled in just one year (2010), as the Chinese restricted supply. Toyota is working hard to develop a new motor that will end its dependence on rare earth metals.

- Switching costs work in their favor. This occurs for a supplier when an industry is tied to it, as for example, the PC industry has been to Microsoft, its dominant supplier of operating systems and software. Switching costs work in the buyer's favor when the buyer can easily drop one vendor for another. The ease with which customers can switch from one airline to another on popular routes makes it hard for airlines to raise prices or cut service levels. Frequent flyer programs were intended to raise switching costs, but they have not been effective.

- Differentiation works in their favor. When buyers see *little* differentiation in the industry's products, they have the power to pit one vendor against another. As the PC itself has become more of a commodity, buyer power has grown. But the PC industry's suppliers (Microsoft and Intel) are highly differentiated. Makers of PCs are squeezed in the middle, caught between powerful suppliers and powerful buyers.

- They can credibly threaten to vertically integrate into producing the industry's product itself. Producers of beer and soft drinks have used this tactic to keep a lid on the prices of beverage containers.

Substitutes

Substitutes—products or services that meet the same basic need as the industry's product in a different way—put a cap on industry profitability. Tax preparation software, for example, is a substitute for a professional tax preparer such as H&R Block. Substitutes place a ceiling on the prices incumbents can sustain without eroding sales. For decades, OPEC, the Organization of the Petroleum Exporting Countries, has fended off substitutes by carefully managing the price of oil to discourage investment in alternative forms of energy. This is why environmentalists favor higher gas taxes.

> Substitutes—products or services that meet the same basic need as the industry's product in a different way—put a cap on industry profitability.

Precisely because substitutes are not direct rivals, they often come from unexpected places. This makes substitutes difficult to anticipate or even to see once they appear. The threat of substitution is especially tricky when it comes at one remove. Over the next generation, for example, electric cars may (or may not!) become a significant substitute for those powered by combustion engines. If they do, this will have a cascading effect, causing substitution in many other parts of the car. Batteries add weight to a vehicle, for example, so BMW is looking at carbon fiber as a lighter substitute for the steel used in car bodies. Companies that make or service transmissions and exhaust systems could well become the buggy whip makers of the twenty-first century.

How do you assess the threat of a substitute? Look to the economics, specifically to whether the substitute offers an attractive price–performance trade-off relative to the industry's product. Coin-star's Redbox—the kiosk that dispenses movie rentals for just $1—has become a tangible threat to Hollywood's ability to sell movie DVDs at twenty to forty times that price. Redbox is a *substitute* for buying videos, and it is a *direct rival* to local video rental stores that can't match the convenience or low cost of Redbox's locations. (Note: About a month after I wrote the last sentence, Blockbuster, once the leading store operator, filed for bankruptcy protection.) While DVD rentals have long been a substitute for buying them outright, Red-box's combination of rock bottom prices and convenience has clearly hit a customer sweet spot.

The sweet spot isn't always the lower-priced alternative. The Madrid–Barcelona high-speed train is a higher-value, higher-price substitute for flying. Energy drinks are a higher-price substitute for coffee. Both drinks are caffeine delivery systems, but some con-sumers will pay more for the substitute's bigger jolt.

Switching costs play a significant role in substitution. Substitutes gain ground when buyers face low switching costs, certainly the case with movie DVDs or, to cite another example, with moving from a branded drug to a generic one. Given that coffee drinking is such a deeply ingrained habit, it's no surprise that energy drinks are more readily adopted by the young.

New Entrants

Entry barriers protect an industry from newcomers who would add new capacity and seek to gain market share. The threat of entry damp-ens profitability in two ways. It caps prices, because higher industry prices would only make entry more attractive for newcomers. At the same time, incumbents typically have to spend more to satisfy their customers. This discourages new entrants by raising the hurdle they would have to clear in order to compete. In a business like specialty coffee retailing, for example, where entry barriers are low, Starbucks must constantly invest to refresh its stores and its menus. If it slacks off, it effectively opens the door for a new rival to join the fray.

Entry barriers protect an industry from newcomers who would add new capacity.

How do you size up the threat of new entry? If you are a current player, what can you do to raise those barriers? If you are thinking of entering a new industry, can you overcome the barriers that stand in your way? There are a number of different kinds of entry barriers. Start with the following questions to help you identify and assess them.

- Does producing in larger volumes translate into lower unit costs? If there are *economies of scale*, at what volumes do they kick in? The numbers matter. Where do these economies come from: From spreading fixed costs over a larger volume? From using more efficient technologies that are scale dependent? From increased bargaining power over suppliers? It costs about a billion dollars to develop a new operating system for a PC, costs that are recovered in a matter of weeks if you have Microsoft's scale.

- Will customers incur any *switching costs* in moving from one supplier to another? Switching from a Mac to a PC, or vice versa, will cost you many hours of setup and relearning. Because Apple has been the small player with low market share, it has had much more to gain from luring customers away from Microsoft. Therefore Apple has invested substantially in reducing those switching costs for PC users.

- Does the value to customers increase as more customers use a company's product? (This is called a *network effect*.) As with economies of scale on the supply side, try to understand where the value comes from and what it's worth. Sometimes the perceived stability or reputation of the company makes it a "safe" choice; sometimes value may come from the size of the network, as it does with Facebook.

- What is the price of admission for a company to enter the business? How large are the *capital investments*, and who might be willing and able to make them? Drug companies haven't worried much about the threat of new entrants, and have therefore been free to raise prices, because the business has historically required such massive investment in R&D and marketing.

- Do incumbents have advantages independent of size that new entrants can't access? Examples include proprietary technology, well-established brands, prime locations, and access to distribution channels. The latter, for example, can be a formidable entry barrier, especially if distribution channels are limited and the industry incumbents have them locked up. This can drive new entrants to create their own channels. For example, the upstart discount airlines had to sell tickets via the Internet because travel agents tended to favor the established airlines.

- Does government policy restrict or prevent new entrants? In my state of Massachusetts, licenses to sell wine are very hard to come by, severely limiting new entrants. Regulations, policies, patents, and subsidies can also work indirectly, by raising or lowering the other entry barriers.

- What kind of retaliation should a potential entrant expect should it choose to enter the industry? Is this industry known for making it tough for newcomers? Does the industry have the resources to compete aggressively? If industry growth is slow or if the industry has high fixed costs, incumbents will typically fight hard to retain their share of the market.

Rivalry

When rivalry among the current competitors is more intense, profitability will be lower. Incumbents will compete away the value they create by passing it on to buyers in lower prices or dissipating it in higher costs of competing. Rivalry can take a variety of forms: price competition, advertising, new product introductions, and increased customer service. Drug companies, for example, have a history of intense competition in R&D and in marketing, but they have steered clear of price competition.

> If rivalry is intense, companies compete away the value they create, passing it on to buyers in lower prices or dissipating it in higher costs of competing.

How do you assess the intensity of rivalry? Porter notes that it is likely to be greatest if

- The industry is composed of many competitors or if competitors are roughly equal in size and power. Often an industry leader has the ability to enforce practices that help the whole industry.

- Slow growth provokes battles over market share.

- High exit barriers prevent companies from leaving the industry. This happens, for example, if companies have invested in specialized assets that can't be sold. Excess capacity typically hurts an industry's profitability.

- Rivals are irrationally committed to the business; that is, financial performance is not the overriding goal. For example, a state-owned enterprise might be propped up for reasons of national pride or because it provides jobs. Or, a corporation may feel its image requires a full product line.

Price competition, Porter warns, is the most damaging form of rivalry. The more rivalry is based on price, the more you are engaged in competing to be the best. This is most likely when

- It is hard to tell one rival's offerings from another (the problem of competitor convergence we saw in chapter 1) and buyers have low switching costs. This typically drives rivals to lower their prices to attract customers, a practice that has dominated airline competition for many years.

- Rivals have high fixed costs and low marginal costs, creating the pressure to drop prices because any new customer will "contribute to covering overhead." Again, the essence of airline economics.

- Capacity must be added in large increments, disrupting the industry's supply–demand balance and leading to price cutting to fill capacity.

- The product is perishable, an attribute that applies not only to fruit and fashion but also to a wide range of products and services that quickly become obsolete or lose their value. A hotel room, an airline seat, or a restaurant table that goes unfilled is "perishable."

Why Only Five Forces?

The five forces framework applies in all industries for the simple reason that it encompasses relationships fundamental to all commerce: those between buyers and sellers, between sellers and suppliers, between rival sellers, and between supply and demand. Think about it. This covers all of the bases. The five forces are universal and fundamental.

> The five forces framework applies in all industries for the simple reason that it encompasses relationships fundamental to all commerce.

When I lead strategy discussions among managers, I usually ask them if they know Porter's five forces framework. Most do. But then something interesting happens. The conversation quickly degenerates into a competition to see who can name all five. Typically, people are only able to remember three or four. Also typically, they will throw in a candidate that isn't one of the five forces, but they're absolutely certain it must be for the simple reason that in *their* industry, this particular phenomenon is highly relevant to their success.

So let me underline the big idea here. Memorizing the five forces won't make you a better business thinker; it will only help you to sound like one. It matters that you grasp the deeper point: there are a limited number of *structural* forces at work in every industry that *systematically* impact *profitability* in a *predictable direction*.

Supply and Demand

Everyone has learned at some point in their training about the importance of supply and demand in determining prices. In perfect markets, the adjustment is very sensitive: when supply rises, prices immediately drop to the new equilibrium. In perfect competition there are no profits because price is always driven down to the marginal cost of production. But in practice, very few markets are "perfect." Porter's five forces framework offers a way to think systematically about imperfect markets. If there are barriers to entry, for example, new supply can't simply rush into the market to meet demand. The power of suppliers and buyers, for example, will have direct consequences for prices. And so on.

Other factors may be important, but they are not structural. Consider four that get the most attention:

- *Government regulation* will be relevant to competition if it changes the industry's structure through its impact on one or more of the five forces.

- The same goes for *technology*. If the Internet, for example, makes it easier for customers in an industry to shop around for the best price, then industry profitability will drop because, in this instance, the Internet has changed the industry's structure by increasing the power of buyers.

- Managers often mistakenly assume that a *high-growth industry* will be an attractive one. But growth is no guarantee that the industry will be profitable. For example, growth might put suppliers in the driver's seat, or, combined with low entry barriers, growth might attract new rivals. Growth alone says nothing about the power of customers or the availability of substitutes. The untested assumption that a fast-growing industry is a "good" industry, Porter warns, often leads to bad strategy decisions.

- Finally, *complements* are sometimes proposed as a "sixth force." Complements are products and services used together with an industry's products—for example, computer hardware and software. Complements can affect the demand for an industry's product (would you buy an electric car if you had no place to plug it in?), but like the other factors under discussion—growth, government, technology—they affect industry profitability through their impact on the five forces.

FIGURE 2-2

How the five forces impact profitability

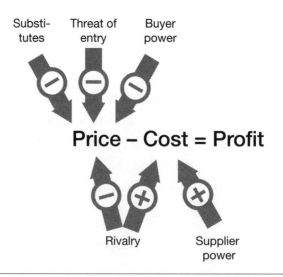

Depending on your industry, then, understanding and managing these factors can be important to your success. But the impact on industry profitability of "more" of any of these factors, unlike "more buyer power," will be neither systematic nor predictable. Some technologies might raise costs and lower prices, therefore lowering profitability. Others might have the opposite effect. Still others will have no impact at all. The same goes for growth, for government, and for complements. If a force is structural, you can always predict that "more" will affect prices or costs in a known direction. More buyer power always drives prices down, not up. More supplier power always pushes costs higher, not lower. Figure 2-2 summarizes the dominant impact on profitability of each of the five forces.

Implications for Strategy

The collective strength of the five forces matters because it affects prices, costs, and the investment required to compete. Industry structure determines how the economic value created by an industry is divided—how much is captured by companies in the industry versus customers, suppliers, distributors, substitutes, and potential new entrants. Industry structure can be linked directly to the income statements and balance sheets of every company in the industry. The insights gained from this kind of analysis should lead directly to decisions about where and how to compete.

How can you use industry analysis? Consider two representative examples. First, does the industry offer the possibility of attractive returns? In 2005, IBM sold its PC business to Lenovo. A five forces analysis makes clear immediately why the business had become so unattractive that even one of its marquee players decided to throw in the towel. Its two superpower suppliers, Microsoft and Intel, cap-

---

Typical Steps in Industry Analysis

1. **Define the relevant industry by both its product scope and geographic scope.** What's in, what's out? This step is trickier than most people realize, so give it some real thought. The five forces help you draw the boundaries, avoiding the common pitfall of defining the industry too narrowly or too broadly. Are you facing the same buyers, the same suppliers, the same entry barriers, and so forth? Porter offers this rule of thumb: where there are differences in more than one force, or where differences in any one force are large, you are likely dealing with distinct industries. Each will need its own strategy. Consider these examples:

   - **Product scope.** Is motor oil used in cars part of the same industry as motor oil used in trucks and stationary engines? The oil itself is similar. But automotive oil is marketed through consumer advertising, sold to fragmented customers through powerful channels, and produced locally to offset the high logistics costs of small packaging. Truck and power generation lubricants face a different industry structure—different customers and selling channels, different supply chains, and so on. From a strategy perspective, these are distinct industries.

   - **Geographic scope.** Is the cement business global or national? Recall the CEMEX example discussed earlier.

---

tured almost all of the value the industry created. And as the industry matured, the PC itself had become a commodity, giving customers more power. Since one beige box was as good as another, customers could easily switch brands in order to get a good price. Rivalry among

> Although some elements are the same, buyers are radically
> different in the United States and Mexico. The geographic
> scope is national, not global, and CEMEX will need a sepa-
> rate strategy for each market.
>
> 2. **Identify the players constituting each of the five forces and, where
>   appropriate, segment them into groups.** On what basis do these
>   segments emerge?
>
> 3. **Assess the underlying drivers of each force.** Which are strong?
>   Which are weak? Why? The more rigorous your analysis, the
>   more valuable your results.
>
> 4. **Step back and assess the overall industry structure.** Which forces
>   control profitability? Not all are equally important. Dig deeper
>   into the most important forces in your industry. Are your results
>   consistent with the industry's level of profitability today and
>   over the long term? Are the more profitable companies better
>   positioned in relation to the five forces?
>
> 5. **Analyze recent and likely future changes for each force.** How are
>   they trending? Looking ahead, how might competitors or new
>   entrants influence industry structure?
>
> 6. **How can you position yourself in relation to the five forces?** Can
>   you find a position where the forces are weakest? Can
>   you exploit industry change? Can you reshape structure in
>   your favor?

PC makers was intensifying, with more price pressure coming from
emerging Asian producers. To top it off, a new generation of potential
substitutes was taking off—a range of mobile devices that had some
of the same functionality as PCs.

Five forces analysis is used most often to determine the "attractiveness" of an industry, and this is certainly indispensible for companies and investors deciding whether to exit, enter, or invest in an industry. But using five forces analysis simply to declare that an industry is attractive or unattractive misses its full power. This use stops short of vital insights into the following questions:

- Why is current industry profitability what it is? What's propping it up?

- What's changing? How is profitability likely to shift?

- What limiting factors must be overcome to capture more of the value you create?

In other words, a good five forces analysis allows you to see through the complexity of competition, and it opens the way to a host of possible actions you can take to improve performance. As unattractive as the PC business is for most of its players, Apple appears to have found a way to make money. By designing its own operating system, Apple has never been subject to Microsoft's supplier power. By creating distinctive products, it has limited buyer power. Apple loyalists would rather pay more than switch.

A second representative question is, Can you position your company where the forces are weakest? Consider the strategy developed by heavy-truck maker Paccar. This is another industry with an uninviting structure:

- There are many big, powerful buyers who operate large fleets of trucks; they are price sensitive because trucks represent a large piece of their costs.

- Rivalry is based on price because (a) the industry is capital intensive, with cyclical downturns, and (b) most trucks are built to regulated standards and therefore look the same.

- On the supplier side, unions exercise considerable power, as do the large independent suppliers of engines and drive train components.

- Truck buyers face substitutes for their services (rail, for example), which puts an overall cap on truck prices.

Between 1993 and 2007, the industry average return on invested capital (ROIC) was 10.5 percent. Yet over the same period Paccar, a company with about 20 percent of the North American heavy-truck market, earned 31.6 percent. Paccar has developed a positioning within this difficult industry where the forces are the weakest. Its target customer is the individual owner-operator, the guy whose truck is his home away from home. This customer will pay more for the status conferred by Paccar's Kenworth and Peterbilt brands and for the ability to add a slew of custom features such as a luxurious sleeper cabin or plush leather seats. Paccar's made-to-order products come with a number of accompanying services geared to make the owner-operator more successful. For example, Paccar's roadside assistance program limits downtime, a key to the owner's economics. In an industry marked by price competition, Paccar is able to charge a 10 percent price premium.

Paccar doesn't try to compete by being the "best" truck maker in the industry. If it did, it would go after the same customers with the same products. It would get caught up in the industry's price competition, intensifying rivalry, which, in turn, would cause further deterioration in industry structure. The lesson here is relevant to many companies in many industries: by your own choices in how you compete, you can easily make a bad situation worse.

Competing to be unique, meeting different needs or serving different customers, lets Paccar run a different race. The forces affecting its prices and costs are more benign. "Strategy," Porter writes, "can be viewed as building defenses against the competitive forces or finding a position in the industry where the forces are weakest." As Paccar illustrates, good strategies are like shelters in a storm. Five forces analysis will give you a weather forecast.

Structure Is Dynamic

As some or all of the forces shift over time, industry profitability will follow. Industry structure is dynamic, not static, a point that Porter has to repeat often because there has been a remarkably persistent misconception that industry structure and positioning are static, and therefore irrelevant in a fast-changing world. Since, as I said in my introduction, many people get their Porter second hand, this is a point worth highlighting. To repeat, then, industry structure is dynamic, not static. When you do industry analysis, you are taking a snapshot of the industry at a point in time, but you are also assessing trends in the five forces.

Over time, buyers or suppliers can become more or less powerful. Technological or managerial innovations can make new entry or substitution more or less likely. Choices managers make or changes in regulation can change the intensity of rivalry. In 1970, for example, Walmart was barely a blip on anyone's radar. Today, as the world's most powerful buyer, it is *the* dominant force in industry after industry. In what must be one of the most honest job titles I've ever seen, the company's chief buyer is called "vice president for international purchase leverage." For anyone tracking the five forces, this was not a sudden disruption that happened overnight. It was—for many industries that supply Walmart—a train wreck seen in painfully slow motion. There was plenty of time to prepare, to choose, to act.

In any industry, there is always change. The better your grasp of industry structure, the more likely it is you will spot and exploit new strategic opportunities or moves that could reshape industry struc-

The Five Forces: Competing for Profits

- The real point of competition is earning profits, not taking business away from your rivals. Business competition is about the struggle for profits, the tug-of-war over who gets to capture the value an industry creates.

- Companies compete for profits with their direct rivals, but also with their customers, their suppliers, potential new entrants, and substitutes.

- The collective strength of the five forces determines the average profitability of the industry through their impact on prices, costs, and the investment required to compete. A good strategy produces a P&L better than this industry average baseline.

- Using five forces analysis simply to declare that an industry is attractive or unattractive misses its full power as a tool. Because industry structure can "explain" the income statements and balance sheets of every company in the industry, insights gained from it should lead directly to decisions about where and how to compete.

- Industry structure is dynamic, not static. Five forces analysis can help anticipate and exploit structural change.

ture in your favor. The challenge is to discern the changes that matter. Change that is truly strategic affects the five forces.

Why are some companies more profitable than others? We've just finished part one of the answer: industry structure explains some of the difference. Now we can move on to part two. A company's relative position within its industry—the subject of the next chapter—can account for even more of the difference.

CHAPTER 3

Competitive: Advantage

The Value Chain and Your P&L

N

O TERM IS MORE closely associated with Porter than *competitive advantage*. You hear it in companies all the time, but rarely as Porter intended. Used loosely, as it most often is, it has come to mean little more than anything an organization thinks it is good at. Implicitly, it is the weapon managers count on to prevail against their rivals.

This misses the mark in important ways. For Porter, competitive advantage is not about trouncing rivals, it's about creating superior value. Moreover, the term is both concrete and specific. If you have a real competitive advantage, it means that compared with rivals, you operate at a lower cost, command a premium price, or both. These are the only ways that one company can outperform another. If strategy is to have any real meaning at all, Porter argues, it must link directly to your company's financial performance. Anything short of that is just talk.

> If you have a real competitive advantage, it means that compared with rivals, you operate at a lower cost, command a premium price, or both.

In the last chapter, we saw how the five forces shape the industry's average P&L. Industry structure, then, determines the performance any company can expect just by being an "average" player in its industry. *Competitive advantage* is about superior performance. In this chapter we'll trace the roots of competitive advantage to the value chain, another key Porter framework.

Economic Fundamentals

Competitive advantage is a *relative* concept. It's about *superior* performance. What exactly does that mean? The pharmaceutical company Pharmacia & Upjohn had a seemingly impressive average return on invested capital of 19.6 percent between 1985 and 2002. During the same period, the steel manufacturer Nucor earned around 18 percent. Are these comparable returns? Should you conclude that Pharmacia & Upjohn had the superior strategy?

Not at all. Relative to the steel industry, where the average return was only 6 percent, Nucor was a stellar performer. In contrast, Pharmacia & Upjohn lagged its industry, in which the superior performers earned more than 30 percent. (For an explanation of why Porter uses return on capital, see the box "Right and Wrong Measures of Competitive Success.")

In gauging competitive advantage, then, returns must be measured relative to other companies within the same industry, rivals

FIGURE 3-1

The right analytics: Why are some companies more profitable than others?

A company's performance has two sources:

	INDUSTRY STRUCTURE	**RELATIVE POSITION**
Porter's framework	Five forces	Value chain
The analysis focuses on	Drivers of industry profitability	Differences in activities
The analysis explains	Industry average price and cost	Relative price and cost

If a company has a COMPETITIVE ADVANTAGE, it can sustain higher relative prices and/or lower relative costs than its rivals in an industry.

who face a similar competitive environment or a similar configuration of the five forces. Performance is meaningfully measured only on a *business-by-business* basis because this is where competitive forces operate and competitive advantage is won or lost. Just to keep our terminology straight, for Porter *strategy* always means "competitive strategy" within a business. The business unit, and not the company overall, is the core level of strategy. *Corporate strategy* refers to the business logic of a multiple-business company. The distinction matters. Porter's research shows that overall corporate return in a diversified corporation is best understood as the sum of the returns of each of its businesses. While the corporate parent can contribute to performance (or, as has been known to happen, detract from it), the dominant influences on profitability are industry specific.

Right and Wrong Measures of Competitive Success

What is the right goal for strategy? How should you measure competitive success? Porter is sometimes criticized for not paying enough attention to people, to management's softer side. Yet he is adamant about the importance of setting the right goal, a view that couldn't be more people-centric.

As any manager knows, goals—and how performance is measured against them—have a huge impact on how people in organizations behave. Goals affect the choices managers make. Although managerial psychology has never been the central focus of Porter's work, this insight about behavior informs his thinking. Start out with the wrong goal—or with goals defined in a misleading way—and you will likely end up in the wrong place.

Performance, Porter argues, must be defined in terms that reflect the economic purpose every organization shares: to produce goods or services whose value exceeds the sum of the costs of all the inputs. In other words, organizations are supposed to use resources effectively.

The financial measure that best captures this idea is return on invested capital (ROIC). ROIC weighs the profits a company generates versus *all* the funds invested in it, operating expenses and capital. Long-term ROIC tells you how well a company is using its resources.* It is also, Porter points out, the only measure that

* Note that the time horizon for evaluating ROIC will vary depending on the investment cycle that characterizes the industry. In the aluminum industry, for example, where it can take eight years to bring a new smelter on-line, the appropriate time horizon is probably a decade. In contrast, three to five years is more appropriate for many service businesses. In a business with little capital, other measures of effective resource use may be required. For example, a consulting firm might measure returns per partner.

matches the multidimensional nature of competition: creating value for customers, dealing with rivals, and using resources productively. ROIC integrates all three dimensions. Only if a company earns a good return can it satisfy customers in a sustainable way. Only if it uses resources effectively can it deal with rivals in a sustainable way.

The logic is clear and compelling. Yet when companies choose their goals—or when they accept the goals financial markets impose on them—this basic logic is often nowhere to be seen. When Porter questions why so few companies are able to maintain successful strategies, he often points to flawed goals as the culprit:

- Return on sales (ROS) is used widely, although it ignores the capital invested in the business and therefore is a poor measure of how well resources have been used.

- Growth is another widely embraced goal, along with its sister goal, market share. Like ROS, these fail to account for the capital required to compete in the industry. Too often companies pursue unprofitable growth that never leads to superior return on capital. As Porter notes wryly when he talks to managers, most companies could instantly achieve rapid growth simply by cutting their prices in half.

- Shareholder value, measured by stock price, has proven to be a spectacularly unreliable goal, yet it remains a powerful driver of executive behavior. Stock price, Porter warns, is a meaningful measure of economic value only over the long run. (For more on this, see Porter's comments in the interview at the end of this book.)

As Southwest Airline's former CEO Herb Kelleher observes, flawed goals such as these lead to bad decisions. "'Market share has nothing to do with profitability,' he says. 'Market share says we just want to be big; we don't care if we make money doing it. That's what misled much of the airline industry for fifteen years, after deregulation. In order to get an additional 5 percent of the market, some companies increased their costs by 25 percent. That's really incongruous if profitability is your purpose.'"

Porter's solution to this problem requires some courage: the only way to know if you are achieving the ultimate goal of creating economic value is to be brutally honest about the true profits you've earned and all the capital you've committed to the business. Strategy, then, must start not only with the right goal, but also with a commitment to measure performance accurately and honestly. That's a tall order, not because it's technically challenging, but because the overwhelming tendency in organizations is to make results look as good as you possibly can.

The same logic applies to nonprofits. Even though they operate in a world without market prices, and therefore without literal profits, the measure of performance should be the same: Does this organization use resources effectively? Measuring performance in the social sector is an equally tall order, one that is not undertaken as often or as rigorously as it should be.

If you have a competitive advantage, then, your profitability will be sustainably higher than the industry average (see figure 3-1). You will be able to command a higher *relative* price or to operate at a lower *relative* cost, or both. Conversely, if a company is less profitable than its rivals, by definition it has lower relative prices or higher relative costs, or both. This basic economic relationship between relative price and relative cost is the starting point for understanding how companies create competitive advantage.

From here Porter takes us through a thought process that's a lot like peeling an onion. First, disaggregate the overall profitability number into its two components, price and cost. This is done because the underlying causal factors, the drivers of price and cost, are so different, and the implications for action are different as well.

Relative Price

A company can sustain a premium price only if it offers something that is both unique and valuable to its customers. Apple's hot, must-have gadgets have commanded premium prices. Ditto for the high-speed Madrid-to-Barcelona train and the trucks Paccar creates for owner-operators. Create more buyer value and you raise what economists call *willingness to pay* (WTP), the mechanism that makes it possible for a company to charge a higher price *relative to rival offerings*.

For many years, U.S. automakers could sell basic passenger cars only by offering substantial rebates or other financial incentives relative to companies such as Honda and Toyota. In 2010, a wave of new products from Ford was beginning to end that long-standing relative price disadvantage. The new Ford Fusion was a top pick of auto critics at *Motor Trend* and *Consumer Reports*, winning praise for quality and reliability. Car buyers seemed to agree. Of the record $1.7 billion Ford earned in the third quarter of 2010, Ford attributed $400 million to higher prices.

In industrial markets, value to the customer (which Porter calls *buyer value*) can usually be quantified and described in economic terms. A manufacturer might pay more for a piece of machinery because, compared with lower-priced alternatives, it will produce offsetting labor costs that exceed the higher price.

With consumers, buyer value may also have an "economic" component. For example, a consumer will pay more for prewashed salad in order to save time. But rarely do consumers actually figure out what they are paying for convenience, in the way a business customer would. (I once calculated, for example, that consumers were effectively paying well over $100 an hour for the unskilled labor involved in grating cheese.)

A consumer's WTP is more likely to have an emotional or intangible dimension, whether it is the trust engendered by an established brand or the status associated with owning the latest electronic gadget. Automakers are betting that consumers will pay a price premium for hybrid cars that well exceeds their potential savings from lower fuel costs. Clearly, noneconomic factors are at work in this calculation.

The same is true in a small but growing corner of the food business. Why are consumers increasingly willing to pay price premiums of three or four hundred percent for what has long been a basic commodity, a carton of eggs? There are a variety of explanations, all of them related to a growing awareness of how eggs are produced on factory farms. For the health-conscious customer, the added value is food safety. For the farm-to-table enthusiast, it's better taste. For the animal ethicist, it's the humane treatment of the hens that lay the eggs.

The ability to command a higher price is the essence of *differentiation*, a term Porter uses in this somewhat idiosyncratic way. Most people hear the word and immediately think "different," but they might apply that difference to cost as well as to price. For example, "Ryanair's low costs differentiate it from other airlines." Marketers have their own definition of differentiation: it's the process of establishing in customers' minds how one product differs from others. Two brands of yogurt may sell for the same price, but you're told that Brand A has "50 percent fewer calories."

Porter is after something different. He is focused on tracking down the root causes of superior profitability. He is also trying to encourage more precise and rigorous thinking by underscoring the distinction between price effects and cost effects. For Porter, then, *differentiation* refers to the ability to charge a higher relative price. My advice here: Don't get hung up on the language, as long as you don't get sloppy about the underlying distinction. Remind yourself that the goal of strategy is superior profitability and that one of its two possible components is relative price—that is, you are able to charge more than your rivals charge.

Relative Cost

The second component of superior profitability is relative cost—that is, you manage somehow to produce at lower cost than your rivals. To do so, you have to find more efficient ways to create, produce, deliver, sell, and support your product or service. Your cost advantage might come from lower operating costs or from using capital more efficiently (including working capital), or both.

Dell Inc.'s low relative costs up through the early 2000s came from both sources. Vertically integrated rivals, such as Hewlett-Packard, designed and manufactured their own components, built computers to inventory, and then sold them through resellers. Dell sold direct, building computers to customer orders using outsourced components and a tightly managed supply chain. These competing approaches had very different cost and investment profiles. Dell's model required little capital since the company did not design or make components, nor did it carry much inventory. In the late 1990s, Dell had a substantial advantage in days of inventory carried. Because component costs were then dropping so fast, buying components weeks later, as Dell effectively did, translated into lower relative costs per PC. And Dell's customers actually paid for their PCs *before* Dell had to pay its suppliers. Most companies have to finance the working capital they need to run their business. Dell's strategy resulted in *negative* working capital, which further enhanced Dell's cost advantage.

Sustainable cost advantages normally involve many parts of the company, not just one function or technology. Successful cost leaders multiply their cost advantages. They are not just "low-cost producers"—a commonly used phrase that implies that cost advantages come only from the production area. Typically, the culture of low cost permeates the entire company, as it does with companies as diverse as Vanguard (financial services), IKEA (home furnishings), Teva (generic drugs), Walmart (discount retailing), and Nucor (steel manufacture). Not only has Nucor historically achieved cost advantages in production, for example, but for years it ran a multibillion-dollar company out of a corporate headquarters about the size of a dentist's office. The "executive dining room" was the deli across the street.

The big idea here is this: strategy choices aim to shift relative price or relative cost in a company's favor. Ultimately, of course, it's the spread between the two that matters: any strategy must result in a favorable relationship between relative price and relative cost. A distinct strategy will produce its own unique structure. One strategy might, for example, result in 20 percent higher costs but 35 percent higher price. Companies such as Apple or BMW lean in that direction. Another strategy might lead to 10 percent lower costs and 5 percent lower price. Companies such as IKEA and Southwest have chosen this kind of structure. Where the net result of the configuration is positive, the strategy has, by definition, created competitive advantage. For Porter, thinking in such precise, quantifiable terms is essential because it ensures that strategy is economically grounded and fact based.

> Strategy choices aim to shift relative price
> or relative cost in a company's favor.

The same big idea applies to nonprofits as well. Remember, competitive advantage is fundamentally about superior value creation, about using resources effectively. Strategy choices for nonprofits aim to shift relative value or relative cost in society's favor. In other words, a good strategy would enable a nonprofit to produce more value for society (the analogue of higher price) for every dollar spent, or to produce as much value using fewer resources (the equivalent of lower cost). To apply Porter's ideas in a nonprofit setting, keep in mind that the nonprofit's goal is to meet a specific social objective with the greatest efficiency. On this score, for-profit managers have it easier. Market prices give them a clear yardstick against which to measure the value they create. Nonprofit managers face the same task, creating value, but without the clarity of that yardstick.

The Value Chain

We now have a concise, concrete definition of competitive advantage: superior performance resulting from sustainably higher prices, lower costs, or both. But we have to peel one final layer of the onion to arrive at what I'll call the managerially relevant sources of competitive advantage—the things that managers can control. Ultimately, all cost or price differences between rivals arise from the hundreds of *activities* that companies perform as they compete.

We need to slow down here for a minute because this is really important and because this language is not intuitive for most managers. Since I'm going to be referring to *activities* and *activity systems* a lot, let's be clear about the definition. *Activities* are discrete economic functions or processes, such as managing a supply chain, operating a sales force, developing products, or delivering them to the customer. An activity is usually a mix of people, technology, fixed assets, sometimes working capital, and various types of information.

Managers tend to think in terms of functional areas such as marketing or logistics because that is how their own expertise or organizational affiliation is defined. That's too broad for strategy. To understand competitive advantage, it is critical to zoom in on activities, which are narrower than traditional functions. Alternatively, managers think in terms of skills, strengths, or competences (what the company is good at), but that's too abstract and often too broad as well. To think clearly about actions you can take as a manager to impact prices and costs, you need to get down to the activity level where "what the company is good at" gets embodied in specific activities the company performs.

The sequence of activities your company performs to design, produce, sell, deliver, and support its products is called the *value chain*. In turn, your value chain is part of a larger *value system*.

The sequence of activities your company performs to design, produce, sell, deliver, and support its products is called the *value chain*. In turn, your value chain is part of a larger *value system*: the larger set of activities involved in creating value for the end user, regardless of who performs those activities. An automaker, for example, has to equip a car with tires. This involves a number of *upstream* choices: Do you make the tires yourself or buy them from a supplier? If you make them yourself, do you buy raw materials from a supplier or do you produce them yourself? Henry Ford famously chose to operate his own rubber plantation in Brazil in the late 1920s, a decision that did not turn out too well. Ultimately, choices like this, about how vertically integrated you want to be, are choices every company makes about "where to sit" in the value system.

There are also activity choices to be made looking *downstream* in the value system. In the 1920s, when cars were still rich men's toys, General Motors and other automakers started their own consumer finance divisions to help customers buy cars on credit. Henry Ford, a man of strong convictions, believed that credit was immoral. He refused to follow GM's lead. By 1930, 75 percent of cars and trucks were bought "on time," and Ford's once dominant market share had plummeted. In thinking about your value chain, then, it's important to see how your activities have points of connection with those of your suppliers, channels, and customers. The way *they* perform activities affects *your* cost or *your* price, and vice versa.

The value chain is another Porter framework that managers refer to all the time. Most, I believe, know what a value chain is—the metaphor of a series of linked activities is intuitive. But many miss the "so what." Why does it matter? The answer: The value chain is a powerful tool for disaggregating a company into its strategically relevant activities in order to focus on the sources of competitive advantage, that is, the specific activities that result in higher prices or lower costs (or, if your organization is a nonprofit, the activities that result in higher value for those you serve or lower costs in serving them).

Key Steps in Value Chain Analysis

The best way to appreciate this tool is actually to use it. Here's how.

1. **Start by laying out the industry value chain.** Every established industry has one or more dominant approaches. These reflect the scope and sequence of activities that most of the companies in that industry perform, and this is as true for nonprofits as for any business. The industry's value chain is effectively its prevailing business model, the way it creates value (see figure 3-2). It is where most

FIGURE 3-2

The value chain: Configuring activities to create customer value

- How far upstream or downstream do the industry's activities extend?

- What are the key value-creating activities at each step in the chain?

- Compare the value chains of rivals in an industry to understand differences in prices and costs

companies in the industry have chosen "to sit" in relation to the larger value system.

How far upstream do the industry's activities extend? Does the industry do basic research? Does it design and develop its products? Does it manufacture? What key inputs does it rely on? Where do they come from? How does the typical player in the industry market, sell, distribute, deliver? Is financing or after-sales service a part of the value the industry creates for customers?

Depending on the industry, some categories will be more or less important in competitive advantage. The key here is to lay out the major value-creating activities *specific to* your industry. If there are competing business models, lay out the value chain for each one. Then look for differences among rivals.

2. **Next, compare your value chain to the industry's.** You can use a template like the one used in the example in this section. The goal is to capture every major step in the value-creating process. For illustrative purposes, I've chosen an example from the nonprofit world, which has the advantage of simplicity. In chapter 4 we'll examine several more complex business value chains. The framework applies equally well in both worlds.

Consider that a number of U.S.-based nonprofits provide wheelchairs to people with disabilities in developing countries. One strategy, which I'll call the "refurbisher," consists of three major activities and looks something like this (figure 3-3):

- **Product sourcing.** Used chairs donated by hospitals, individuals, and manufacturers are collected and then refurbished.

- **Distribution/delivery.** Wheelchairs are shipped to recipients overseas; an in-country charity or nongovernmental organization distributes the chairs to end users.

- **Custom fitting.** Professionals (typically volunteers) follow the chairs overseas to custom-fit each chair. This service, called *provision*, is important because an ill-fitting wheelchair can create its own health issues.

FIGURE 3-3

Donated wheelchairs: A value chain example

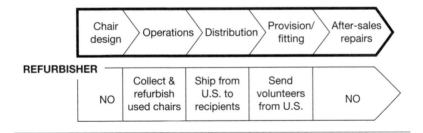

An even simpler strategy, which I'll call the "volume purchaser," consists of just two primary activities: fundraising and buying huge volumes of the most basic, standardized chairs from the lowest-cost producers in China. These are distributed without provision or other user services. Here, the value created is as stripped down as the value chain (figure 3-4): no design, no provision, no repairs.

FIGURE 3-4

Donated wheelchairs: Two competing value chains

	Chair design	Operations	Distribution	Provision/ fitting	After-sales repairs
REFURBISHER	NO	Collect & refurbish used chairs	Ship from U.S. to recipients	Send volunteers from U.S.	NO
VOLUME PURCHASER	NO	Outsource production of low-cost chairs	Ship direct from Asian producer to recipients	NO	NO

Whirlwind Wheelchair International (WWI) takes a different approach, starting with a different way of thinking about the value it wants to create. When founder Ralf Hotchkiss was a college student in 1966, a motorcycle accident left him paralyzed. The first time he took his wheelchair out on the street, he hit a crack in the sidewalk and the chair broke. Hotchkiss, an engineer and a bicycle maker, has spent the last forty years redesigning wheelchairs, not only for his own use but also and especially for people in developing countries where the physical conditions are particularly challenging. His most famous design is called the Rough Rider. Consider Whirlwind's value chain activities (figure 3-5):

- **Product sourcing.** Rather than accept donations of what Hotchkiss calls "hospital chairs," good only for maneuvering indoors, he starts further upstream in order to create true "mobility" chairs. A team of designers based at San Francisco State University works with wheelchair users, designing chairs to fit their lives and withstand local conditions. Adding user-

FIGURE 3-5

Donated wheelchairs: Three competing value chains

	Chair design	Operations	Distribution	Provision/ fitting	After-sales repairs
REFURBISHER	NO	Collect & refurbish used chairs	Ship from U.S. to recipients	Send volunteers from U.S.	NO
VOLUME PURCHASER	NO	Outsource production of low-cost chairs	Ship direct from Asian producer to recipients	NO	NO
WHIRLWIND	YES	Partners produce WWI's designs	Regional producers ship to country partners	Local partners do provision & assembly (P&A)	YES P&A centers handle parts & service

originated design to the value chain creates a higher-value product.

- **Manufacturing.** Whirlwind works with a handful of regional manufacturers outside the United States, partners large enough to achieve efficient scale and sophisticated enough to meet Whirlwind's quality standards.

- **Distribution.** Where feasible, chairs are shipped to the end-use countries flat packed. This cuts shipping costs in half and allows for some local value-added at the final destination. Centers operated by local partners perform final assembly and provision, and they carry spare parts so the wheelchairs can be serviced over time. This extends their useful life and solves a big problem of the refurbisher approach: donated hospital chairs from the United States are next to impossible to repair if parts are needed.

Whirlwind's configuration of activities produces a different kind of value with a different cost profile. Looking at competing value chains side by side highlights those differences. If your value chain looks like everyone else's, then you are engaged in competition to be the best.

3. Zero in on price drivers, those activities that have a high current or potential impact on differentiation. Do you or could you create superior value for your customers by performing activities in a distinctive way or by performing activities that competitors don't perform? Can you create that value without incurring commensurate costs? Buyer value can arise throughout the value chain. It can come from product design, for example, as it does for Whirlwind Wheelchair. It can come from choices in the inputs used or the production process itself, both of which are key to the success of In-N-Out Burger, a chain of over 230 hamburger restaurants that uses only the freshest ingredients and prepares its limited menu on-site. It can be created by the selling experience, as any visitor to an Apple Store will tell you. Or, it can arise from after-sales support activities. Every Apple Store, for example, has a Genius Bar where customers can go for free help with technical questions. Whirlwind's spare parts policy is another example. Whether the customer is a company or a household, examining how your activities are part of the whole value system is the key to understanding buyer value.

4. Zero in on cost drivers, paying special attention to activities that represent a large or growing percentage of costs. Your relative cost position (RCP) is built up from the cumulative cost of performing all the activities in the value chain. Are there actual or potential differences between your cost structure and those of your rivals? The challenge here is to get as accurate a picture as you can of the full costs associated with each activity, including not only direct operating and asset costs but also the overhead costs that are generated because you perform this activity.*

To get a handle on this, you can ask yourself what specific overhead costs could be cut if you stopped performing this activity.

For each activity, a cost advantage or disadvantage depends on cost drivers, or a series of influences on relative cost. The real "so what" of relative cost analysis comes when you dig deep enough into the numbers to uncover the actions you can take to improve them. A full-blown example would fill its own chapter. The brief one provided here will give you a sense of what I mean. Southwest Airlines has long enjoyed a cost advantage, as measured in its low relative cost per available seat mile. To understand why, you would list all of Southwest's activities, assign costs to them, and then compare the results with those of other carriers. Let's follow the trail on just one activity: gate turnarounds. Southwest does it faster, and as a result it gets more out of its assets—its costs per plane and per employee are lower than those of rivals.

Seeing that gate turnarounds are a significant cost driver, you would then dive a level deeper, to the many specific subactivities involved in gate turnarounds. Here you'd be looking for ways to lower your costs without sacrificing customer value. This is how you drive an even greater wedge between your performance and that of your rivals. When a plane lands, for example, the lavatories have to be drained. To do this,

---

*Activity-based costing has been around for decades, but it is admittedly hard to do. Accounting systems don't provide cost data in a form that managers can use to understand relative costs. For further guidance on the analytics of competitive advantage, see the notes for this chapter.

Do You Really Have a Competitive Advantage? First You Quantify, and Then You Disaggregate

1. How does the long-term profitability in each of your businesses stack up against other companies in the economy? In the United States, from 1992 to 2006, the average company earned about 14.9 percent return on equity (earnings before interest and taxes divided by average invested capital less excess cash), although this varied somewhat over the business cycle. Are the returns for your business better or worse? If better, something is working in your favor. If worse, then something is wrong. In either case, dig deeper into the underlying causes.

2. Now compare your performance to the average return in your industry, and do so over the last five to ten years. Profitability can fluctuate in the short run as a result of a number of factors as transient as the weather. Choose a longer time horizon, ideally one that matches the investment cycle of your industry. This will tell you whether or not you have a competitive advantage.

   Suppose company A earns a 15 percent return against a national benchmark of 13 percent and an industry benchmark of 10 percent. The analysis of industry structure will explain why the industry overall is 3 points below the national average. But A's superior performance—it exceeds its industry by 5 points—indicates that it has a competitive advantage. So in this case, A does not have a strategy problem. On the other hand, it does have to deal with a challenging industry structure.

The distinction between these two sources of profitability is crucial because the factors that affect industry structure and those that determine relative position are very different. Until a company understands where its profit performance comes from, it will be ill equipped to deal with it strategically.

3. Next, keep digging to understand why the business is performing better or worse than the industry average. Disaggregate your relative performance into its two components: relative price and relative cost. Relative price and cost are essential for understanding strategy and performance.

   In the example under discussion, company A achieved a 5 percent higher return than the average competitor. Its realized price (adjusting for concessions and discounts) was 8 percent higher than the industry average. To command that premium, company A had to spend more: in this case, its relative cost was 3 percentage points higher. That explains A's 5 percent higher return.

4. Dig further. On the price side, it may be possible to trace the overall price premium (or discount) to differences in particular product lines, in customers or geographic areas, or in list price versus discounts off list. On the cost side, it is often revealing to disaggregate the cost advantage (or disadvantage) into that part due to operating cost (income statement) and that part due to the utilization of capital (balance sheet).

These basic economic relationships underlie company performance and strategy. Strategy is about trying to shape these underlying determinants of profitability.

a piece of equipment is hooked up to a service panel. The problem, Southwest discovered, was that this interfered with the ground crew's other servicing activities. The solution: Southwest got its supplier, Boeing, to reposition the service panel in the new 737-300.

As the Southwest example shows, ferreting out cost drivers can be like detective work. It demands both creativity and rigorous analysis. The easier path is simply to accept the industry's conventional wisdom. Most auto companies in the 1990s, for example, accepted on faith that scale was *the* decisive cost driver, that if you didn't sell at least four million cars a year, your costs would kill you. A frenzy of consolidation, much of it subsequently undone, followed.

Of course, scale matters in the auto industry. But a deeper understanding of the cost drivers is critical. Honda, for example, is a relatively small car company. This might lead you to conclude that Honda would have a cost disadvantage. But Honda is the world's largest producer of motorcycles, and overall it is a huge producer of engines. Since engines account for 10 percent of the cost of a car and Honda can share the cost of engine development across its product lines, this scope advantage offsets its overall lack of scale. Moreover, Honda's focus on engine development is an element of differentiation that supports its pricing.

Strategic Implications: Porter's Brave New World

It is no exaggeration to say that the value chain, first laid out in depth by Porter in *Competitive Advantage* (1985), has changed the way managers see the world. Consider the enormous consequences of value chain thinking.

The first is that you begin to see each activity not just as a *cost*, but as a step that has to add some increment of value to the finished product or service. Over time, this perspective has revolutionized the way organizations define their business. Thirty-five years ago, for example, the brokerage business, with its hefty commissions, was how stocks were traded. One size fit all, or at least it fit those wealthy enough to afford it. Everyone took for granted that the business was what the business was.

You begin to see each activity not just as a *cost*, but as a step that has to add some increment of value to the finished product or service.

But what happens when you start thinking about that business as a collection of value-creating activities? You see that behind that broker was a fully integrated set of activities that ranged all the way from doing research and analysis of securities to executing trades to sending out monthly statements. The costs of all those activities were buried in the price of the commission. Charles Schwab created the company that bears his name—and a new category known as *discount brokerage*—around a different value chain. Not all customers want advice, so why should they have to pay for it? Take away all the activities needed to give advice, focus instead on executing trades, and you can create a different kind of value: low-cost trades that make stock ownership accessible to a wider customer base. Matching the *value chain*—the activities performed inside the company—to the customer's definition of value was a new way of thinking just twenty-five years ago. Today it has become conventional wisdom.

A second major consequence of value chain thinking is that it forces you to look beyond the boundaries of your own organization and its activities and to see that you are part of a larger value system involving other players. For example, if you want to build a fast food business around consistent, perfect French fries, as McDonald's did, you can't make excuses to customers because the potato farmer you buy from lacks proper storage facilities. Customer don't care who's at fault. They care only about the quality of their fries. So, McDonald's has to perform specific activities to make sure that, one way or another, all the potato growers from whom it buys can meet its standards.

And everyone in the value system had better understand the role they play in the larger process of value creation, even when they are removed by one or two steps from the ultimate end user. Most wine drinkers know how unpleasant it can be to uncork a nice bottle of wine, pour it for a guest, and then discover that it's corky—that is, the taste has been ruined by a problem known as cork taint. By the 1990s, the problem reached a tipping point for wine makers and sellers. They wanted cork makers to fix it. You don't want a cheap, commodity-like component to ruin the value of an expensive product.

Cork, most of which comes from trees in Portugal and other Mediterranean countries, has enjoyed a near monopoly on wine closures not just for decades, but for centuries. No surprise, then, that the cork makers were slow to respond. Their skill lay in harvesting cork from the outer bark of cork oaks without damaging the trees. They were hand workers—basically farmers, not chemists.

This created an opportunity for plastics makers such as Nomacorc to step into the breech. Nomacorc's value chain made it relatively easy for it to undertake research into the chemistry of wine taint, and to solve the problem. While the traditional cork makers were stuck in an older mind-set ("we're in the cork business"), the plastics makers could see how to become part of a larger value-creating process. By 2009, Nomacorc's automated North Carolina factory was churning out close to 160 million plastic stoppers a month, and synthetic corks had captured 20 percent of the market.

This interdependence of value chains has enormous implications. Managing *across* boundaries, whether these are between the company and its customers or the company and its suppliers or business partners, can be as important for strategy as managing within one's own company. Using Porter's value chain construct was like looking through a microscope for the first time. Suddenly managers could see a whole world of relationships that had previously been invisible to them.

The value chain was a major breakthrough for analyzing both a company's relative cost and value. The value chain focuses managers on the specific activities that generate cost and create value for buyers. Although managers often talk about how their organization's skills or capabilities create value, activities are where the rubber meets the road. Nomacorc clearly had what most managers would call a "core competence" in chemistry. But its competitive success in the wine market resulted from decisions to deploy those capabilities in activities that enhanced the design and manufacture of wine stoppers.

Can You Execute Your Way to Competitive Advantage?

We now have a complete definition of competitive advantage: a difference in relative price or relative costs that arises because of *differences in the activities* being performed (see figure 3-6). Wherever a company has achieved competitive advantage, there *must be* differences in activities. But those differences can take two distinct forms. A company can be better at performing *the same configuration* of activities, or it can choose *a different configuration* of activities. By now, of course, you recognize that the first approach is competition to be the best. And by now, we are in a better position to understand why this approach is unlikely to produce a competitive advantage.

Porter uses the phrase *operational effectiveness* (OE) to refer to a company's ability to perform similar activities better than rivals. Most

FIGURE 3-6

Competitive advantage arises from the activities in a company's value chain

ACTIVITIES	Perform SAME activities as rivals, execute better	Perform DIFFERENT activities from rivals
VALUE CREATED	Meet same needs at lower cost	Meet different needs and/or same needs at lower cost
ADVANTAGE	Cost advantage, but hard to sustain	Sustainably higher prices and/or lower costs
COMPETITION	Be the BEST, compete on EXECUTION	Be UNIQUE, compete on STRATEGY

managers use the term "best practice" or "execution." Whichever term you prefer, we are talking about a multitude of practices that allow a company to get more out of the resources it uses. The important thing is not to confuse OE with strategy.

First, let's recognize that differences in OE are pervasive. Some companies are better than others at reducing service errors, or keeping their shelves stocked, or retaining employees, or eliminating waste. Differences like these can be an important source of profitability differences among competitors.

But simply improving operational effectiveness does not provide a robust competitive advantage because rarely are "best practice" advantages sustainable. Once a company establishes a new best practice, its rivals tend to copy it quickly. This treadmill of imitation is sometimes called hypercompetition. Best practices spread rapidly, aided by the business media and by consultants who have created an industry around benchmarking and quality/continuous improvement programs. The most generic solutions, those that apply in multiple company and industry settings, diffuse the fastest. (Name an industry that has yet to be visited by some version of Total Quality Management.)

Programs like these are compelling. Managers are rewarded for the tangible improvements they achieve when they implement the latest best practice inside their companies. That makes it all too easy to lose sight of the bigger picture of what's happening *outside* their companies. Competing on best practices effectively raises the bar for everyone. While there is absolute improvement in OE, there is relative improvement for no one. The inevitable diffusion of best practices means that everyone has to run faster just to stay in place.

No company can afford sloppy execution. Inefficiency can overwhelm even the most distinctive and potentially valuable strategies. But betting that you can achieve competitive advantage—a *sustainable* difference in price or cost—by performing *the same activities* as your rivals is a bet you will probably lose. No one has been better at OE competition than the Japanese, but, as Porter's work documents in great detail, OE competition has led even the best of them to chronically poor profitability.

Competitive rivalry, at its core, is a process working against the ability of a company to maintain differences in relative price and relative cost. Competition to be the best is the great leveler. It accelerates that process. In the next four chapters, we will see how strategy, built around a unique configuration of activities, works to achieve and sustain competitive advantage. Strategy is the antidote to competitive rivalry.

The Economic Fundamentals of Competitive Advantage

- Popular metrics such as shareholder value, return on sales, growth, and market share are misleading for strategy. The goal of strategy is to earn superior returns on the resources you deploy, and that is best measured by return on invested capital.

- Competitive advantage is not about beating rivals; it's about creating superior value and about driving a wider wedge than rivals between buyer value and cost.

- Competitive advantage means you will be able to sustain higher relative prices or lower relative costs, or both, than your rivals in an industry. If you have a competitive advantage, it will show up on your P&L.

- For nonprofits, competitive advantage means you will produce more value for society for every dollar spent (the analogue of higher price), or you will produce the same value using fewer resources (the equivalent of lower cost).

- Differences in relative prices and relative costs can ultimately be traced to the activities that companies perform.

- A company's value chain is the collection of all its value-creating and cost-generating activities. The activities, and the overall value chain in which activities are embedded, are the basic units of competitive advantage.

PART TWO

What Is Strategy?

YOU CAN CALL any plan or program a strategy, and that's how most people use the word. But a good strategy, one that will result in superior economic performance, is something else. To recap quickly, competitive advantage means you have created value for customers *and* you are able to capture value for yourself because the positioning you have chosen in your industry effectively shelters you from the profit-eroding impact of the five forces. I realize that last sentence is a mouthful. More simply put, you have found a way to perform better by being different.

Porter's definition of strategy is normative, not descriptive. That is, it distinguishes a *good* strategy from a *bad* one. His focus is on *content*, not *process*. His focus is on *where you want to be*, not on the *decision-making process* by which you got there—not how, or even whether, you do formal strategic planning, nor whether your strategy can be captured in fifty words or less. Others in the field have pursued legitimate and important process and people questions such as those, while Porter has, to use a well-worn strategy phrase, "stuck to his knitting": the general principles of creating and sustaining competitive advantage.

In this section of chapters, we'll cover five tests every good strategy must pass:

- A distinctive value proposition
- A tailored value chain

- Trade-offs different from rivals

- Fit across value chain

- Continuity over time

We'll see how each of these contributes to a strategy and its sustainability over time.

CHAPTER 4

Creating Value:

The Core

STRATEGY'S FIRST TEST, HAVING a distinctive value proposition, is so intuitive that many managers think they have a strategy if they can get this far. Choosing the particular kind of value you will offer your customers is the core of competing to be unique. But recall the definition of competitive advantage: a difference in relative price or relative costs that arises because of *differences in the activities* being performed. Your value chain must be specifically tailored to deliver your value proposition. A value proposition that can be effectively delivered without a tailored value chain will not produce a sustainable competitive advantage. The tailored value chain is Porter's second test, and it is neither obvious nor intuitive.

How these two core elements of strategy are linked to each other—and how they are linked to industry structure and competitive advantage—is the subject of this chapter. Strategy means deliberately choosing a different set of activities to deliver a unique mix of value. If all rivals produce the same way, distribute the same way, service the same way, and so on, they are, in Porter's terms, competing to be the best, and not competing on strategy.

The First Test: A Distinctive Value Proposition

The value proposition is the element of strategy that looks outward at customers, at the demand side of the business. A value proposition reflects choices about the particular kind of value the company will offer, whether those choices have been made consciously or not. Porter defines the value proposition as the answer to three fundamental questions (see figure 4-1):

- Which customers are you going to serve?

- Which needs are you going to meet?

- What relative price will provide acceptable value for customers and acceptable profitability for the company?

FIGURE 4-1

The value proposition answers three questions

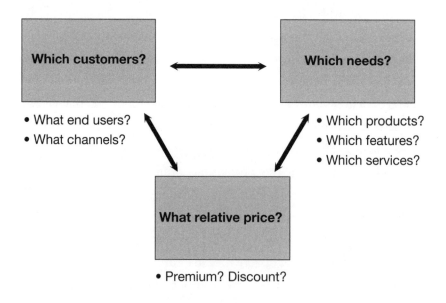

> The value proposition is the element of
> strategy that looks outward at customers, at
> the demand side of the business. The value
> chain focuses internally on operations.
> Strategy is fundamentally integrative, bringing
> the demand and supply sides together.

This definition reflects the evolution of Porter's thinking beyond his 1996 HBR article "What Is Strategy?" There he described three sources of positioning: variety, needs, and access. Subsequent work led him to the more complete formulation discussed here, one he has elaborated over the past decade in numerous speeches and lectures.

Which Customers?

Within an industry, there are usually distinct groups of customers, or customer segments. A value proposition can be aimed specifically at serving one or more of these segments. For some value propositions, choosing the customer comes first. That choice then leads directly to the other two legs of the triangle: needs and relative price.

Customer segmentation is typically part of any good industry analysis, and choosing the customer(s) you will serve can be an important anchor in your positioning vis-à-vis the five forces. In the examples that follow, note how each reflects a different basis for segmentation: Walmart's segmentation was based on geography, Progressive's on demographics, and Edward Jones's on psychographics.

Given that Walmart is the world's largest retailer, with over $400 billion in sales, it may seem irrelevant to ask which segment Walmart serves. But like all large companies, Walmart started small, and it had to pick a place to begin. Choosing to serve a specific customer group gave Walmart its start. In the 1960s, when Walmart began operations, discount retailing was a new, disruptive business model. While the early players focused on big cities and metropolitan areas like New York, Sam Walton did something unique: he chose isolated rural towns with populations between 5,000 and 25,000. Walmart's "key strategy," in Walton's own words, "was to put good-sized stores into little one-horse towns which everybody else was ignoring."

In terms of the five forces, this choice of customers insulated Walmart from direct rivalry with other discounters. Although people tend to think of Walmart as a fierce competitor, Walmart started out by completely avoiding head-to-head competition. Doing so gave it many years of breathing room to develop and extend its positioning as a provider of everyday low prices.

Progressive, the Ohio-based auto insurer, also built a strategy around a customer its industry was largely avoiding. For about three decades, Progressive thrived by choosing to serve what the industry called "nonstandard" drivers, those more likely to be involved in accidents and to file insurance claims (motorcycle owners, for example, or motorists with drunk-driving records). With few alternatives, nonstandard buyers typically had little bargaining power.

Finally, if you look at the wealth management business, you'll find just about everyone chasing the same demographic segment: the high-net-worth individual. Not Edward Jones, one of the consistently most successful U.S. brokerage firms. For thirty years, it has focused on customers defined not by how much money they have, but on their attitude toward investing. Jones serves conservative investors who delegate financial decisions to a trusted advisor. In terms of the five forces, this customer segment has been less price sensitive and more loyal.

As often happens, each of these value propositions targeted a customer group overlooked or avoided by the industry. That's not essential, however. In insurance, for example, USAA has been a stellar performer with a value proposition aimed at low-risk customers. Here's what *is* essential: finding a unique way to serve your chosen segment profitably.

Which Needs?

In many cases, choosing the need the company will serve is the primary decision that leads to the other two legs of the triangle. Here, strategy is built on a unique ability to meet a particular need or a subset of needs. Often that ability arises from the specific features of a product or service. Typically, value propositions based on needs appeal to a mix of customers who might defy traditional segmentation. Instead of belonging to a clear demographic category, the company's customers will be defined by the common need or set of needs they share at a given time.

> Typically, value propositions based on needs appeal to a mix of customers who might defy traditional demographic segmentation.

Enterprise Rent-A-Car is the market leader in car rental services in North America, where it is bigger than the once-dominant players, Hertz and Avis. Enterprise has also been dramatically more profitable. It is the only major company in the industry that has enjoyed sustained superior profitability, because for decades it pursued a distinctive strategy.

The Enterprise value proposition is based on a simple insight: renting a car meets different needs at different times. Hertz and its followers in the industry built their business around travelers, people away from home on business or on vacation. Enterprise recognized that a sizeable minority of rentals, roughly 40 to 45 percent, occur in the renter's home city. If your car is stolen, for example, or damaged in an accident, you'll need a rental. In such cases, your insurance company might cover the cost, usually with contractual limits on the price it will pay. About a third of Enterprise's revenues come from insurers. Other occasions prompt home-city rentals as well—for example, when a car has a mechanical failure or when a child is home from school on vacation. In all of these uses, home-city car renters tend to be more price sensitive than business or vacation travelers.

Enterprise crafted a unique value proposition to meet these needs: reasonably priced, convenient, home-city rentals. Compared with Hertz and Avis, Enterprise has chosen to serve a different need at a different relative price. It is not that Enterprise is the *best* car rental company. Nor is the market it serves inherently better. But starting with the specific need it serves, Enterprise has made a *different* choice about the value proposition triangle. Enterprise's customer base would confound traditional market segmentation by demographic characteristics.

Zipcar, started in Cambridge, Massachusetts, in 2000, is pursuing a different path to uniqueness in home-city car rentals. Its value proposition targets yet another kind of customer with a different kind of need (see figure 4-2). Zipsters, as the company's members are called, are often people who choose not to own a car, but who occasionally need to use one. Zipcar allows them to rent a car for time periods as short as an hour.

FIGURE 4-2

Positioning maps

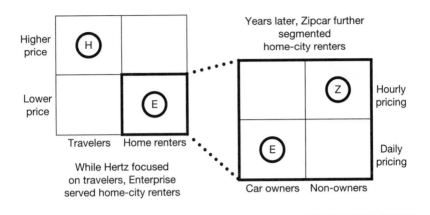

Zipcar offers an interesting and complex mix of value: extreme convenience in vehicle pickup and drop-off; extreme flexibility in the rental period; clear, all-inclusive pricing that includes insurance and gas; and the intangible "cool" factor associated with this fast-growing brand. I should add that because this company is an early work-in-progress, it will undoubtedly continue to test the boundaries of its value proposition and to make adjustments to it as it learns.

What Relative Price?

For some value propositions, relative price is a primary leg of the triangle. Some value propositions target customers who are overserved (and hence overpriced) by other offerings in the industry. A company can win these customers by eliminating unnecessary costs and meeting "just enough" of their needs. At the product level, think about the difference between a bare-bones cell phone and a more expensive, feature-laden smartphone. Where customers are overserved, the lower relative price is often the dominant leg of the triangle.

Conversely, some value propositions target customers who are underserved (and hence underpriced) by other offerings in the industry. Customers who choose NetJets instead of flying first class on a commercial airline, for example, want an enhanced service and are willing to pay a steep premium for it. Similarly, Denmark's Bang & Olufsen (B&O) gives its customers something more than the spectacular sound quality offered by other high-end audio equipment makers. B&O's customers want products that look as good as they sound, and they are willing to pay more for beautiful design. In value propositions like B&O's, the unmet need is typically the dominant leg of the triangle, while the higher relative price supports the extra costs the company has to incur to meet it.

When Needs Are Overserved: Southwest. According to company legend, here's how Southwest Airlines was born. Back in the late 1960s, "a couple of guys said, 'Here's an idea. Why don't we start an airline that charges just a few bucks and has lots of flights every day instead of what the other guys are doing—charging a lot of bucks and having just a few flights each day?'" That, in a nutshell, is Southwest Airlines' value proposition: very low prices coupled with very convenient service.

Southwest Airlines, the most successful—and the most emulated—airline in the world, has thrived by meeting "just enough" of its customers' needs at dramatically lower prices. From its humble beginnings flying only to three cities in Texas in 1971, Southwest has grown to be one of the world's leading airlines, both in size and in profitability. It has done so with a value proposition that for three decades was radically different from other airlines.

Southwest didn't promise to get you anywhere you wanted to go, as other airlines did. Nor did it offer the basic amenities that were once standard industry fare: meals, assigned seats, baggage transfers. Full-service airlines (perhaps a term that no longer accurately describes the legacy carriers, with their higher costs and prices) overserved the needs of a large number of travelers flying Southwest's shorter point-to-point routes.

Southwest's value proposition put it in a unique position vis-à-vis the five forces. As most know, the airline industry is brutally inhospitable.

- Suppliers, especially the labor unions but also plane makers, are powerful.

- Customers are powerful because they are price sensitive and have low switching costs.

- Rivals, dealing with high fixed costs, compete on price to fill seats.

- New entrants are a constant threat, because entry barriers are lower than you might think. You can start an airline with a couple of leased planes.

- Substitutes keep prices down. Customers can choose other forms of transportation, especially on shorter trips.

Southwest's low relative costs provided shelter from the industry's self-destructive price competition. Moreover, its value proposition gave it a truly unique positioning vis-à-vis that last force, substitution. Its low fares made flying an attractive alternative for price-sensitive travelers accustomed to driving or taking a bus. In the early years, a shareholder asked CEO Herb Kelleher if Southwest couldn't raise its prices by just a few dollars since its $15 price on the Dallas–San Antonio route was so much lower than Braniff's $62 fare. Kelleher said no, our real competition is ground transportation, not other airlines.

Consider Southwest's first expansion beyond its original three cities, Dallas, Houston, and San Antonio. It chose Harlingen, Texas, a town in the Rio Grande Valley probably few people have ever heard of. The year before Southwest launched its service, 123,000 passengers flew from Southwest's base cities to the Valley. Within a year after Southwest began flying to Harlingen, passenger volume jumped to 325,000.

And price isn't the whole story. Southwest was also more convenient. First, its frequent departures allowed customers to travel when they wanted. Second, its flights arrived on time and customers didn't have to wait in slow lines at the ticket counter. Third, the secondary airports that became central to Southwest's strategy were closer to downtown, cutting a traveler's total trip time. These convenience factors were a draw for business travelers.

Southwest didn't figure out every element of its value proposition on Day One. Companies rarely do. It learned by doing. Here's a classic example of how that happens in practice. In 1971, one of the planes in Houston needed to go to Dallas for routine maintenance over the weekend. Then-CEO Lamar Muse didn't want to fly the plane empty, figuring that some revenue was better than none. He offered seats on the Friday-night flight for $10, half off the standard $20 fare on that route. The flight sold out, providing some extra cash for the struggling start-up.

Even better than the cash was the game-changing insight about Southwest's customers. Some were clearly more price sensitive, and less time sensitive, than others. Muse acted immediately. He raised the peak fare to $26 and dropped the off-peak fare to $13. Multiple-tier pricing is now standard industry practice, but at the time, it was a major innovation. It allowed Southwest to further segment its customers and to fill its planes. Lower off-peak fares appeal to leisure travelers who are more price sensitive and have greater flexibility about when they travel than do business passengers.

Thus Southwest's value proposition cut across traditional customer segments, appealing, on given occasions, to a variety of customers: business travelers, families, and students. Instead of meeting all of the needs of a target customer all of the time, Southwest meets one type of need that many customers have at least some of the time. Southwest created a distinct kind of value that, for many decades, distinguished it from other airlines.

Although Southwest has been widely imitated, it would be a mistake to say that Southwest has found the "best" value proposition for the industry. It is only "best" at meeting a particular kind of need at a particular relative price.

When Needs Are Underserved: Aravind Eye Hospital. India's Aravind Eye Hospital was founded in 1976 by an idealistic retired army surgeon, Govindappa Venkataswamy, known as Dr. V. Dr. V. didn't need a detailed market segmentation map to identify a large population with a dramatically underserved need. Millions of Indians suffer from preventable blindness because they can't afford cataract surgery. Starting with just eleven beds and three doctors, Aravind has become the world's largest provider of eye care in the world, performing about 300,000 surgeries a year, at least two-thirds of them for free.

Aravind has an extraordinary value proposition. Correction: it has *two* value propositions. One is aimed at affluent customers who want the best eye care money can buy. These customers want to be seen by state-of-the-art doctors in state-of-the-art facilities, and they are willing to pay the going market rate for such advanced medical care. That's one value proposition.

The second is for those who can't afford to pay and who would otherwise become blind. Aravind offers them sight, and the independence that goes with it. The medical care is identical to that provided to the paying patients—same doctors, same operating rooms. The hotel function (room and board) is vastly stripped down. But the price is stripped down even further, all the way to zero.

Aravind has thrived by meeting vitally important needs for two distinct customer segments, at different price points. What's most remarkable is that Aravind is financially self-sustaining—it depends neither on government money nor on charitable donations, although its success has increasingly attracted the latter. Instead it has a strategy that has proven to be sustainable for over three decades.

The first test of a strategy is whether your value proposition is different from your rivals. If you are trying to serve the same customers *and* meet the same needs *and* sell at the same relative price, then by Porter's definition, you don't have a strategy.

In most businesses, there are many different possible configurations of the value proposition triangle. Some companies serve virtually all customers in the market but only meet a specific need or cluster of needs. Other companies serve a more focused customer base but aim to meet more of those customers' needs. Some companies deliver higher value at a premium price. Others, enabled by their efficiency, offer a low relative price.

The first test of a strategy is whether your value proposition is different from your rivals. If you are trying to serve the same customers *and* meet the same needs *and* sell at the same relative price, then by Porter's definition, you don't have a strategy. You're competing to be the best.

The Second Test: A Tailored Value Chain

If you're trying to describe a strategy, the value proposition is a natural place to begin. It's intuitive to think of strategy in terms of the mix of benefits aimed at meeting customers' needs. But the second test of strategy is often overlooked because it is not intuitive at all. A distinctive value proposition, Porter explains, will not translate into a meaningful strategy unless the best set of activities to deliver it is different from the activities performed by rivals. His logic is simple and compelling: "If that were not the case, every competitor could meet those same needs, and there would be nothing unique or valuable about the positioning."

Insight into customers' needs is important, but it's not enough. The essence of strategy and competitive advantage lies in the *activities*, in choosing to *perform activities differently* or to *perform different activities* from those of rivals. Each of the companies we've just described has done just that, tailoring their value chains to their value propositions.

Walmart, Progressive, and Edward Jones

Let's return to the trio of companies whose value propositions were built around serving a distinct customer. We'll begin our look at tailored value chains by simply highlighting the major activity choices that reflect each company's chosen segment, and how those choices are different from those made by rivals who are serving different customers.

First, Walmart. While other discounters chose to put stores in large metropolitan areas, Walmart invested in small-town locations, where the nearest city was probably a four-hour drive away. Walton knew this terrain well. He rightly bet that if his stores could match or beat those city prices, "people would shop at home." Moreover, many of Walmart's markets were too small to support more than one large retailer. This was a powerful barrier to entry. By being first, Walton was able to preempt competitors and discourage them from entering Walmart's territory, allowing the company time to hone the enduring sources of its competitive advantage: its ability to provide everyday low prices in markets all across the country and beyond.

Progressive's target customer posed a special challenge. How do you turn a bad driver into a profitable customer? Progressive needed a different value chain from the industry's standard one. First, Progressive tackled risk assessment in a different way, building a massive database with more granular indicators that better predicted the probability of accidents. It used this data to spot the good risks in pools that looked like bad drivers to other insurers. For example, among drivers cited for drinking, those with children were least likely to reoffend; among motorcyclists, Harley owners aged forty-plus were likely to ride their bikes less often. Progressive used information like this to set prices so that even the worst customers could be profitable. Progressive's competitive advantage, then, started with relative price (for comparable risks).

Second, since accidents were likely, Progressive focused on minimizing their cost once they occurred. The faster claims were settled, for example, the more money Progressive could save. (Less time meant fewer lawsuits.) Progressive's value chain accomplished this in a number of ways. Most dramatically, an adjuster equipped with a company van and a laptop could go directly to the accident scene and issue a check on the spot. This was not common practice in the industry. Progressive's competitive advantage, then, also had a component of lower relative cost.

Like Progressive, Edward Jones also tailored its value chain to its chosen customer segment, conservative individual investors who wanted a trusted advisor to make financial decisions for them. Trust is built through personal, face-to-face relationships. To that end,

Jones invests in conveniently located offices, and lots of them—in small towns, suburbs, and strip malls. Each office has just one financial advisor, a model unique in the industry. Jones prefers to hire from outside the industry, looking for advisors with both community and entrepreneurial spirit. It spends heavily on training new hires in its conservative product line (mostly blue-chip investments) and its buy-and-hold philosophy.

Jones pays a price for these activities tailored to its chosen customer. It foregoes revenue from more frequent trading or more exotic investments with higher margins. Its training and its occupancy costs are high relative to other brokerage firms. But these activities create value for Jones's chosen customers, who are willing to pay a large premium ($100 per trade versus $8 for low-priced brokers) for Jones's trusted personal touch.

Aravind's Value Chain

The original inspiration for Aravind came from, of all places, McDonald's. Dr. V. wanted to produce cataract surgeries as efficiently and as consistently as McDonald's produced hamburgers. He designed a system that does just that.

Essentially, while a surgeon is operating on one patient, the next patient is already prepped on a table behind him. When one operation ends, the surgeon simply turns around and starts the next one. Not a minute of the skilled surgeon's valuable time is lost. Everyone in the operating room, including the surgeon, is trained to follow a standardized procedure. Every step in the process is carefully integrated to produce an efficient whole.

The results speak for themselves: Aravind, in 2009–2010, performed about 5 percent of all eye surgeries in India, employing only 1 percent of the nation's ophthalmic manpower. The achievement mirrors that of Henry Ford's assembly line for the Model T, which made Ford workers five times more productive than the auto industry average. Aravind has made cataract surgery affordable by applying the core design elements that Ford used to make cars affordable for the masses: standardization of activities, specialization of labor and equipment, and a high-volume production line that never stops.

The operating model drives Aravind's ability to create value, but it's not the whole story. After all, what good is being a low-cost producer in a market where even low cost is too expensive? Dr. V.'s solution: charge paying customers market rates. Because Aravind's costs are so much lower than other providers, each paying customer subsidizes free care for two. That, very roughly speaking, is the arithmetic of Aravind's competitive advantage.

Aravind's value chain choices support its ability to attract paying customers, who are housed in a separate wing or building that offers every modern comfort. The real draw, however, is the quality of the medical care. Aravind is professionally state of the art. It has developed a premier teaching and research institute, with affiliations with leading eye centers around the world. Its doctors are world class.

Those of you who understand the challenges faced by hospital administrators are now probably shaking your heads. How do you get surgeons to agree to be treated like assembly line workers? A five forces analysis of this industry would tell you that surgeons have all the leverage to demand shorter hours, higher pay, and more autonomy. Yet Aravind is able to do something that continues to elude health-care delivery in the United States. Aravind tracks costs, time, and results—even postsurgical outcomes—all of which can be traced back to specific doctors and the data used to help them improve their performance.

There is a glib answer for how Dr. V. was able to find doctors willing to accept these conditions. His original hires were family members. They simply couldn't say no. There is a more serious answer as well. Dr. V. has built an organization that offers two powerful nonmonetary rewards. One is its commitment to professional development and excellence. Consider, for example, the extensive training it provides and its professional affiliations. The second is an appeal to selfless service and compassion. This is an organization on a mission. And that mission, as intangible as it sounds, contributes to Aravind's competitive advantage in tangible ways. Aravind's values allow it to recruit and retain the talent it needs and to configure its activities in an extraordinary way—a way that is perfectly tailored to its value proposition.

Aravind provides quality eye care at a price everyone can afford. That's its value proposition. Its tailored value chain turns that promise into a strategy.

Southwest's Tailored Activities

Comparing high-minded Aravind to fun-loving Southwest Airlines may feel like a stretch, but strategically speaking they have a lot in common, and a lot to teach about strategy. Both have produced sustained superior performance in the face of difficult industry conditions.

Like Aravind, Southwest has cultivated a service culture that makes its strategy work. The company spent most of its early years fighting legal battles that threatened its very survival. The existing carriers in Texas did not want a low-priced competitor to enter the market. They used every legal and political weapon money could buy to prevent Southwest from flying. This intensified the sense of mission at Southwest, creating a distinctive "warrior" culture dedicated to freeing travelers from the grips of a customer-unfriendly industry. Southwest's employees, like Aravind's, go the extra mile. Though unionized, they have never adopted the adversarial, zero-sum attitude toward the company that has plagued other airlines. This contributes to competitive advantage, raising customer satisfaction and lowering relative costs. Both Southwest and Aravind, for example, benefit from low turnover.

Before Southwest's success shook up the airline industry, most carriers pursued a common way of competing, imitating each other's hub-and-spoke systems, pricing structures, frequent flyer programs, and union agreements. Southwest chose not to pursue these industry "best practices"—some of them valid ways of competing that meet other needs on other types of routes. Instead, Southwest has created a tailored configuration of activities to deliver its unique outcome.

The traditional full-service airline is designed to get passengers from almost any point A to any point B. To reach a large number of destinations and serve passengers with connecting flights, full-service airlines employ a hub-and-spoke system centered on major airports. To attract passengers who desire more comfort or services, they offer first class or business class. To accommodate passengers who must change planes, they coordinate schedules and check and transfer baggage. Because some passengers will be traveling for many hours, full-service airlines traditionally served meals.

Southwest, in contrast, tailored all its activities to deliver frequent service on its particular type of route at the lowest cost. From the start, it didn't offer meals, assigned seats, interline baggage checking, or premium classes of service, all of which contributed to the faster gate turnaround times we saw in chapter 3. This enables Southwest to keep planes flying longer hours and to provide frequent departures with fewer aircraft. Gate and ground crews are leaner, more flexible, and more productive than its rivals. A standardized fleet of aircraft boosts the efficiency of maintenance. As Web-based travel sites became a popular distribution channel, most airlines rushed to sign up (a bad decision for industry structure, since it pushes customers to buy on price alone). Not Southwest. Its passengers buy tickets directly on the Southwest Web site, bypassing other channels and allowing Southwest to avoid sales commissions.

These are just some of the cost drivers underpinning Southwest's competitive advantage, allowing it to serve more passengers per employee, to get more daily departures per gate, and to get more hours of use per plane. Southwest staked out a unique and valuable strategic position based on a tailored set of activities. On the routes served by Southwest, a full-service airline could never be as convenient or as low cost.

A strategic positioning, especially when it has a high degree of focus, is sometimes seen as carving out a "niche." The implication of that word is that the market opportunity is small. Although this may sometimes be the case, even focused competitors can be very large. In the case of Southwest, what initially looked like a narrow niche has revolutionized the airline industry. Both Southwest and our next example, Enterprise Rent-A-Car, have become industry leaders.

Car Rental Value Chains

Enterprise's unique value proposition—rentals for car owners in their home city—is only part of the story of its success. The choices it has made in configuring its value chain explain its competitive advantage. Enterprise was able to serve customers who wanted lower costs because those needs could be met with a different, lower-cost configuration of activities. Enterprise's strategic insight was that its particular value proposition would *require* a completely different value chain from a Hertz or an Avis.

Other car rental companies chose high-rent locations convenient to travelers, for example, airports, train stations, or hotels. Not Enterprise. It chose small offices, often simple storefronts, spread all over a metropolitan area, a practice that began when founder Jack Taylor started his tiny auto leasing business in St. Louis in 1957. But as the

Can You Be Differentiated and Low Cost at the Same Time?

Early in his career, Porter identified a set of generic strategies—focus, differentiation, and cost leadership—that quickly became one of the most widely used tools for thinking about key strategic choices. Each of the three reflects the most basic level of consistency that every effective strategy must have. *Focus* refers to the breadth or narrowness of the customers and needs a company serves. *Differentiation* allows a company to command a premium price. *Cost leadership* allows it to compete by offering a low relative price. These broad characterizations of strategy types capture the fundamental dimensions of strategic choice relevant in any industry.

At the same time, Porter described a common strategic mistake, which came to be known as getting stuck in the middle. This happens when a company tries to be all things to all customers and is outflanked by cost leaders on one side, who meet "just enough" of their customers' needs, and by differentiators on the other side, who do a better job of satisfying customers who "want more" (of some particular attribute they value).

company grew and its strategy emerged, so did the strategic logic. Nothing could be more inconvenient for a home-city renter than to have to go to the airport to pick up a car.

What began as an accident of early company history became a matter of strategic choice. For its chosen customer, Enterprise's neighborhood locations, now within fifteen miles of 90 percent of the U.S. population, are more convenient. The rent was also lower, allowing Enterprise to charge lower prices than rivals. Only in 1995, more than thirty-five years after the company was founded, did Enterprise

Does this mean that a company can't be both differentiated and low cost at the same time? Not at all, although this is another persistent misconception. Porter's earliest work (circa 1980) is sometimes cited as evidence to the contrary. But Porter went on in the 1990s to refine his work on the link between the value proposition and the value chain, work that should have put that misunderstanding to rest. "When you get down to the specific needs that are served by specific products," he explains, "you see that the possible choices/combinations are far more complex. Generic strategies identified one dominant theme of a strategy, such as relative cost. But effective strategies integrate multiple themes in a unique way. Customers' needs are rarely uni-dimensional and therefore a strategy to meet those needs won't be uni-dimensional either. When a company makes choices about which customers and needs it will serve, and when it tailors its value chain to those choices, it is possible to be differentiated and low cost and focused at the same time, as Enterprise is. Or, like Southwest, you can be more convenient and lower cost—without getting stuck in the middle."

open its first airport location. In the car rental business, it is easy to see that the optimal configuration of offices is very different for travelers than for home-city renters.

In fact, positive-sum competition is possible precisely because there are a variety of ways to configure most activities. Zipcar is able to do away with offices entirely. Zipsters are paid members whose information is on file, eliminating all the usual paperwork of a rental transaction. Technology makes customer service staff unnecessary because Zipsters make reservations online. Zipcars are parked in designated spots spread throughout a metro area. Special access Zipcards with embedded wireless chips allow members to open the specific car they've reserved only at the specified rental time. Transponders on the windshield record hours of usage and mileage, which are directly communicated to a central computer via a wireless link. Zipcar makes renting a car as easy as withdrawing cash from an ATM.

Other parts of the value chain are tailored as well. Every car rental company has to configure its fleet of vehicles. Because vacation and business travelers often want special car models—SUVs or convertibles, for example—Hertz and Avis include these "hot" vehicles in their fleets. Enterprise's home-city renters are satisfied with lower-cost, more basic models. They are also less concerned with the age of a car, enabling Enterprise to keep its cars longer than the traveler-oriented companies. Zipcar is building its brand with a fleet of "cool" cars like the environmentally friendly Honda Insight and the BMW Mini.

For Zipcar, the cars themselves, displaying the company's hip logo, are like rolling billboards that announce the company's brand to the neighborhood. Zipcar also attracts new customers through a raft of partnerships with schools and companies. In keeping with its value proposition, Enterprise tends to market to insurance companies and car dealerships, another important way in which its costs are kept low. In contrast, Hertz uses expensive consumer advertising to attract its business and leisure travelers.

When a company focuses on delivering a different kind of value to a different set of customers—for Porter, the essence of strategic positioning—the list of value chain differences can be extensive (see figure 4-3).

Limits Are Essential

Choices in the value proposition that limit what a company will do are essential to strategy because they create the opportunity to tailor

FIGURE 4-3

Each value proposition is best delivered by a tailored value chain

	Hertz	Enterprise	Zipcar
Value proposition			
Customer/need	Travelers away from home; rent by the day	Replacement cars at home; rent by the day	Cars for non-owners at home; rent by the hour
Pricing	Premium: expense accounts or vacation travel	Economy: insurance or self-pay	Varies by usage: subscription plus hourly fee
Value chain choices			
Office locations	Airports, hotels, train stations ($$$)	Throughout metro area, strip malls ($)	None (¢)
Fleet choices	Full range of late models	"Sensible" cars, older fleet	"Cool" cars
Marketing	Consumer advertising ($$$)	Market through body shops, insurers ($)	Word of mouth, partnerships with schools (¢)

activities in a way that best delivers that kind of value. Tailoring is possible only if there are limits, only if you are not trying to be all things to all people. In other words, limits make it possible to develop a value chain that is different from that of rivals who have chosen to offer a different kind of value.

> Choices in the value proposition that limit what a company will do are essential to strategy because they create the opportunity to tailor activities in a way that best delivers that kind of value.

This is a crucially important test that should be applied to any strategy. If the same value chain can deliver different value propositions

Discovering New Positions: Where to Begin

"Strategic competition," Porter writes, "can be thought of as the process of perceiving new positions that woo customers from established positions or draw new customers into the market." In describing a strategy *after the fact*, the value proposition is the logical place to begin, as I have done in this chapter. But how do companies, in practice, actually find new positions? Looking for new ways to segment customers or to serve unmet needs is one starting point. But the value chain—the unique set of activities your company performs—is an equally valid starting point. This, in fact, is essentially what companies do when they identify their "strengths."

Consider Grace Manufacturing, a small, family-owned company based in Arkansas. Grace is not a household name, but its leading product, the Microplane, is renowned among cooks as the tool of choice for grating hard cheeses and zesting citrus. The Microplane, followed by tens of line extensions, created a new segment in the housewares industry.

How Grace discovered its position is an interesting story. The company was a contract manufacturer of steel printer bands, a product approaching obsolescence as printer technology advanced. Facing the imminent demise of its core product, Grace's principal asset was a proprietary masking and etching process that produced

equally well, then those value propositions have no strategic relevance. Only a value proposition that requires a tailored value chain to deliver it can serve as the basis for a robust strategy. This is the first line of defense against rivals.

Strategy, then, defines a way of competing, reflected in a set of activities that delivers unique value in a particular set of uses or for a bands with razor-sharp edges. Chris Grace, now the company's CEO, recalled working in the family business while he was in high school: "'Back then, if you worked in the plant, it wasn't a question of whether you were going to cut your finger, but when. We realized we were good at making sharp things. And so we thought, what can we make that's sharp?'" They settled on tools for serious woodworkers.

The Microplane brand rasp was designed to be mounted on a hacksaw frame. But somehow word got out that it made an extraordinary kitchen tool. Richard Grace, the company's founder, was initially disappointed when he heard how his product was being used. But today, the company makes a whole line of sharp products for the kitchen, from pizza cutters to chocolate graters. Moreover, leveraging its proprietary know-how in producing sharp things, Grace has added products for orthopedists that grind bone or prepare hip sockets for implants. *Proprietary* is a key word in this story. Grace Manufacturing didn't just have a strength in making sharp things. Most essential for strategy, it had a *unique* strength.

Discovering new positions is a creative act. What triggers the initial insight often varies from one person, and one organization, to the next. No cookbook or expert system can reliably churn out winning strategies. By definition, strategy is about creating something unique, making a set of choices that nobody else has made.

particular set of customers, or both. In most industries, there can be many strategically relevant value propositions. This simply reflects the great diversity in customers and needs, and the fact that different activity configurations are often required to meet those needs most effectively. Even when an industry produces something that looks like a homogenous product, Porter points to many opportunities up and down the value chain for differentiation—in delivery, in disposal, in certification and testing, and in financing, to name just a few dimensions.

While not every single activity need be unique, robust strategies always involve a significant degree of tailoring. To establish a competitive advantage, a company must deliver its *distinctive value* through a *distinctive value chain*. It must perform different activities than rivals or perform similar activities in different ways.

Thus the value proposition and the value chain—the two core dimensions of strategic choice—are inextricably linked. The value proposition focuses externally on the customer. The value chain focuses internally on operations. Strategy is fundamentally integrative, bringing the demand and supply sides together.

CHAPTER 5

Trade-offs:

The Linchpin

IN THE LAST CHAPTER, I presented Porter's first two tests of strategy: a unique value proposition and the tailored value chain required to deliver it. If there is one important takeaway message, it is that strategy requires choice. Competitive advantage depends on making choices that are different from those of rivals, on making trade-offs. This is Porter's third test. Trade-offs play such a critical role that it's no exaggeration to call them strategy's linchpin. They hold a strategy together as they contribute to both creating and sustaining competitive advantage.

The need to make trade-offs is yet another idea that runs counter to popular thinking, and it does so in two ways. The first misconception is about trade-offs themselves. Managers tend to believe that "more is always better." More customers, more products, more services mean more sales and profits. You can have it all. You can do *both* A and B. If you choose either one or the other, you'll be leaving money on the table. Making trade-offs is almost a sign of weakness.

The second misconception is about whether it is possible, in today's supercharged, hypercompetitive world, to *sustain* a competitive advantage. This is a world in which anything can and will be copied, a world in which the best you can hope for in competing is a series of very temporary advantages. Sound familiar? This is, once again, competing to be the best.

But think about it for a minute, and you'll see that this argument fails to square with the facts. It's true that choosing a unique value proposition alone is no guarantee of sustainability. If you find a valuable position, imitators will take notice. But competitive advantages can and do persist for decades, as companies such as Southwest Airlines, IKEA, Walmart, Enterprise Rent-A-Car, BMW, McDonald's, Apple, and many others attest. What do the strategies of such diverse companies as these have in common? The answer lies in just one word: *trade-offs*.

What Are Trade-offs?

Trade-offs are the strategic equivalent of a fork in the road. If you take one path, you cannot simultaneously take the other. Whether the fork in the road is about the characteristics of the product itself or about the configuration of activities in the value chain, a trade-off means that you can't have it both ways because the choices are incompatible.

> Trade-offs are the strategic equivalent of a fork in the road. If you take one path, you cannot simultaneously take the other.

Every airline, for example, must choose a route system. It can choose a hub-and-spoke configuration that offers passengers the ability to travel between many more destinations but at higher cost, or it can choose a point-to-point route system that sacrifices "ubiquity," serving fewer destinations but doing so at lower cost. The choice is a stark either-or. An airline can choose one or the other, but it can't choose both at once without creating inefficiencies.

Where there are trade-offs, products or activities are not just different. They are inconsistent. One choice precludes or compromises the other. Competition is full of economic trade-offs. These lie at the very heart of strategy.

Consider Taiwan Semiconductor (TSMC), a semiconductor manufacturer with sales of about $9 billion (in 2009). While most entrepreneurs are known for coming up with new products or services, Morris Chang, the founder of Taiwan Semiconductor, built a company by recognizing the value of a single, crucial trade-off. When he started TSMC in 1987, nearly all of the major semiconductor companies were what the industry calls integrated device manufacturers (IDMs). That is, they designed and manufactured their own chips. Because the manufacturing facilities for chips are very expensive, if the IDMs had excess capacity, they would rent it out to smaller firms that couldn't afford to build their own facilities. For the IDMs, the needs of these smaller companies were just an afterthought.

Dr. Chang knew that this situation posed a real dilemma for the smaller companies. On the one hand, they couldn't afford their own capacity. On the other hand, by outsourcing production to the IDMs, they put at risk their most valuable asset, their intellectual property. They lived in fear that an IDM would steal their chip designs.

Morris Chang was willing to make a big trade-off. He would become a manufacturer for other chip designers. Period. Taiwan Semiconductor would not be in the business of designing its own chips. With that one crucial choice, Dr. Chang eliminated the conflict of interest. Instead of competing with his customers, he would simply manufacture for them. By so doing, he would create more value for his customers. And, of course, this fundamental policy choice meant that TSMC had a different value chain than its rivals— its activities were different.

This trade-off was the source of TSMC's competitive advantage. And remember that competitive advantage is not just something you're good at, it's something that's reflected in your P&L. By focusing only on manufacturing, Morris Chang achieved lower relative costs (that is, his manufacturing costs were lower than those of rival IDMs). And because he offered intellectual property protection in addition to manufacturing, customers were willing to pay more for the added value he created.

Robust strategies typically incorporate multiple trade-offs. The very best have trade-offs at almost every step in the value chain. Consider IKEA, the Swedish home furnishings giant. IKEA's value proposition is to provide good design and function at a low price. Its target customer is what IKEA calls the person "with a thin wallet." In choosing its particular kind of value and the activities needed to deliver it, IKEA has accepted a set of limits: it does *not* meet *all* the needs of *all* customers.

In every major value-adding step in the process of creating and selling home furnishings, IKEA has made different choices from what I'll call the "traditional" home furnishings retailer. Consider the following:

- **Product design.** IKEA's furniture is modular and ready to assemble. The traditional retailer sells fully assembled pieces. That's a critical either-or trade-off. Either a piece of furniture is fully assembled or it isn't. Unlike most other companies in its industry, IKEA designs its own products; this choice then allows IKEA to make all kinds of critical trade-offs in styling and in the cost of everything it sells. IKEA's designers are given very specific targets with clear constraints: design a coffee table for a given product line that will sell for $30. Here's where you see some sharp trade-offs. You can have good design at low cost, but there is no way you can have, for example, a $30 coffee table made of birdseye maple, or a $40 chair made with the finest leather. IKEA's designers are tasked with making clear trade-offs regarding each product.

- **Product variety.** Traditional retailers offer a wide range of furniture styles—from American colonial to French country to Ming dynasty. They offer customers hundreds of fabric choices. But both breadth and customization add costs. IKEA's trade-off: carry a narrow style range, limited to Scandinavian and its offshoots, and offer only a few choices of finishes and fabrics. In turn, trade-offs that limit product complexity allow IKEA to source product in bulk from efficient third-party manufacturers that produce on a global scale. Remember the five forces. IKEA is a Goliath, able to negotiate favorable prices from its suppliers.

- **In-store service.** Traditional retailers use sales associates to help customers with the hundreds of choices involved in furnishing a home. Sales associates, however, add cost. Here is another sharp trade-off, an either-or choice. Either you staff a store with sales associates or you don't, but you can't have it both ways. IKEA is explicit about this trade-off. It tells its customers that in exchange for serving themselves, they will be rewarded with lower prices. Even the store cafeteria reinforces this message. Signs explain that clearing your own table at the end of your meal allows the low price you paid at its start.

- **Delivery and store design.** Traditional furniture sellers have products shipped direct from a manufacturer or a warehouse to the customer's home. IKEA explicitly "outsources" delivery to its customers, again in exchange for lower prices. Its many trade-offs in store design and location make it easy (well, as easy as it can be) for you to serve yourself. When you see something you like in one of IKEA's many, many room displays, you write down the item number. As you leave the last display area and before you arrive at the checkout lines, you pass through a cavernous warehouse, its shelves stacked with ready-to-assemble furniture in flat packs. You look for your item number, load the flat pack onto IKEA's specially designed shopping cart, and out you go to your car. IKEA chooses car-friendly locations (in the United States, never downtown) with ample free parking; it creates huge stores to display and stock every item (never small stores displaying only selected items).

- **Flat packs and competitive advantage.** Early in IKEA's history, or so the story goes, an IKEA employee removed the legs of a table so that a customer could carry it home in his car. As the company tells it, this was one of those Eureka moments. If furniture were sold disassembled and in flat packs, customers could "self-deliver." In addition, the space-saving flat packs massively lower the cost of logistics. IKEA can fit six times the number of pieces into each truckload being delivered to its stores.

  This insight ultimately became a source of competitive advantage; that is, it led to differences in the activities in IKEA's value chain that resulted in lower costs than those of its rivals. Shipping costs for furniture in flat packs are dramatically lower than those for assembled furniture. This allows IKEA to charge lower prices and still make a profit.

  Flat packs have other advantages. Customers who are willing to carry their purchases home and do their own assembly not only pay a lower price, but also get the furniture today, without waiting weeks for delivery, and with far less risk of shipping damage. This adds to IKEA's cost advantage, and it enhances customer satisfaction. I've never forgotten the first sofa I ever bought. After waiting six weeks for it to be delivered, it arrived with a big tear in the fabric. I spent hours arranging to have the sofa shipped back to the manufacturer, and another six weeks waiting for the replacement. Not a happy experience for me, and a costly one for the vendor.

An intriguing recent study has found a so-called IKEA effect: that self-assembly actually raises, not lowers, the price consumers would be willing to pay. Not bad when you can raise customer value and lower your own costs at the same time!

Now think about the cumulative impact of these differences in cost and value, all of them stemming from one trade-off: either you sell fully assembled furniture that has to be shipped, *or* you design it to be transported in flat packs and assembled in-home by the customer. Porter is fond of saying that if you have a strategy, you should be able to link it directly to your P&L. This is an example of precisely that kind of linkage.

> If you have a strategy, you should be able to
> link it directly to your P&L.

Tailored choices pervade IKEA's value chain. And many of those choices about how to create its distinctive form of value are not just different from the choices its rivals make. They are incompatible—that is, a rival couldn't copy what IKEA does without compromising or damaging the value it creates for its customers. These are genuine either-or choices that allow IKEA to deliver on its value proposition—good design at low cost.

Why Do Trade-offs Arise?

Trade-offs arise for a number of reasons. Porter highlights three. First, product features may be incompatible. That is, the product that best meets one set of needs performs poorly in addressing others. IKEA's huge stores are a nightmare for those who want to make a quick "in and out" purchase. BMW's "ultimate driving machine" does not serve the needs of car buyers looking for cheap, basic transportation. McDonald's fast, cheap hamburgers are not very satisfying for locavores who want healthy, farm-fresh ingredients.

Second, there may be trade-offs in activities themselves. In other words, the configuration of activities that best delivers one kind of value cannot equally well deliver another. You can bet that a plant designed to handle small lot sizes and custom products will be less efficient for large production runs or standard products. A logistical system geared to deliver once per hour is not the best one to deliver once per week. And so on. Trade-offs like these have economic consequences. If an activity is either overdesigned or underdesigned for its use, value will be destroyed. If you've had the pleasure of being served by a concierge at a Four Seasons hotel, you know that the company designs this "activity" to provide guests with a high level of assistance. It costs money to create this kind of value, hiring and training the right kind of person. If you put that same concierge in a setting where some guests require little or no assistance, then some of the cost that went into creating that high level of service would be wasted.

Another source of trade-offs is inconsistencies in image or reputation. Can you imagine, for example, the Italian sports car maker

Ferrari introducing a minivan? Companies have occasionally been blinded to such inconsistencies in image by their zeal to expand. For decades, the retailer Sears built a reputation as *the* place to buy quality tools and appliances. When it acquired broker Dean Witter and tried to sell investment products as well as power saws, customers just couldn't reconcile the new image of Sears with the old. The result was one of the more spectacular failures in the history of corporate expansion. At best, inconsistencies like these confuse customers. At worst, they undermine the company's credibility and reputation.

Trade-offs, then, arise for many reasons. They are pervasive in competition. They make strategy possible by creating the need for choice.

Real Trade-offs Keep Imitators at Bay

If you are successful and competitors aren't asleep at the switch, they will try to copy what you do. But trade-offs will get in their way. By their very nature, trade-offs are choices that make strategies sustainable because they are not easy to match or to neutralize. If there are no trade-offs, any good idea can be copied. Product features can be copied. Services can be copied. Ways of delivering value can be copied. But where there are trade-offs, the copycat will pay an economic penalty.

Not-So-Fast Food

McDonald's, a market leader in fast food, built its positioning around speed and consistency. Everything in its value chain is tailored to deliver that value proposition. But in the late 1990s,

McDonald's had a growth problem. Coming off a series of failed product launches and facing market saturation, McDonald's decided that it needed to match rivals Burger King and Wendy's by offering customers the option to customize their menu options (for example, a burger without the pickles). The company introduced its "Made for You" campaign, which involved expensive refurbishing of the kitchens at all its restaurants. The total bill was estimated at close to half a billion dollars.

But "Made for You" came with other costs as well. Customized food preparation takes more time, and the greater the customization, the more difficult it is to achieve consistency. If you're starting to think that each of these outcomes—speed, consistency, customization—involves trade-offs, you're paying attention. More customization equals less speed and less consistency. Moreover, preparing each order at the time of purchase deprived restaurants of the ability to stock up for the busy lunch hour. Beleaguered franchises found themselves between a rock and a hard place: they could take a profit hit by hiring extra workers to staff the kitchens, or they could risk irritating customers with long waits. McDonald's learned about trade-offs the hard way. It couldn't copy Burger King's strategy without messing up its own.

Porter calls what McDonald's tried to do *straddling*, and it is the most common form of competitive imitation. The straddler, as the word implies, tries to match the benefits of the successful position while at the same time maintaining its existing position. In other words, a straddler tries to have it all, to get the best of two worlds by grafting new features, services, or technologies onto the activities it already performs. Strategy is an either-or realm; the straddler thinks it can escape into a world of both-and. This usually turns out to be wishful thinking.

Movies: Direct Versus Retail

The more common outcomes are cases like Blockbuster. The largest operator of video rental stores in the United States, Blockbuster was threatened by the growing success of Netflix, whose subscribers ordered movies online for home delivery via mail, and, as the technology evolved, via direct download as well. These are two different value propositions requiring two different value chains, with significant trade-offs. Netflix's 50-plus regional warehouses, backed by a state-of-the art distribution system, could supply a wider library of films than Blockbuster's 5,000-plus local stores. Blockbuster tried— and failed—to have it both ways, adding Netflix's value proposition on top of its own. Trade-offs impose real economic penalties for companies that try to compete in two ways at once.

Straddling in the Skies

When British Airways (BA) set out to defend its turf against the rising tide of budget carriers, it had the advantage of hindsight. Most recently, there had been several notable straddling fiascos in the industry, including Continental Airlines' attempt to be full service on some routes and low cost on others. Competing in two ways at once turned out to be too expensive and too complicated.

British Airways took this lesson to heart: if you're going to occupy two distinct positions in the same business, the only way to bypass the trade-offs is to create a separate organization with the freedom to choose its own, tailored value chain. BA's experience shows that even when you do that, it is still a very hard act to pull off.

Its new subsidiary, Go Fly, was allowed to establish an independent identity, with its own management team, branding, and route

The Cost/Quality Trade-off: True or False?

"You get what you pay for" is a phrase that captures one of the oldest and most fundamental trade-offs in business thinking: to create higher quality, you need to incur higher costs; conversely, if you cut costs, you will reduce quality. This was an obvious and eternal truth . . . until, that is, it was seemingly shown to be false by the quality movement in the 1980s and 1990s. That movement, with its rallying cry "Quality Is Free," first took hold in Japan and then spread to the rest of the world. Company after company found that they could reduce costs and improve quality at the same time. It appeared to many that a fundamental trade-off could be broken.

Can you have high quality and low cost at the same time? Is quality free? Porter calls this a "dangerous half-truth." The answer is "Yes, *but*." Yes, quality is free when higher quality means eliminating defects and waste. There you are dealing with a false trade-off, one that should be broken. In general, false trade-offs arise when organizations fall behind in operational effectiveness—that is, when they lag in how well they perform basic activities, the kind of activities that are generic and not strategy specific. Thus, in the 1990s, Lexus was able to offer "more luxury" than Cadillac at a lower price because General Motors had fallen so far behind the current state of best practice. Today, in U.S. health care, where I believe there is great opportunity to improve medical outcomes and reduce costs at the same time, the slogan "Quality Is Free" might serve as a useful wake-up call.

It is also the case that innovations come along and render old trade-offs obsolete. Innovations such as new technologies and new management practices can result in both lower cost and improved performance. But only when such innovations change the game—or when a company is lagging in efficiency to begin with—is it true that quality is free.

Once companies achieve parity in execution, however, they face real trade-offs. Then, adding "quality" usually means adding new features, using better materials, or offering greater service. In a passenger car, for example, it might mean upgrading from cloth seats to leather, or adding a global positioning system. Quality in that sense of the word is definitely not free. It almost always costs more to add significant product features, improve service, provide better sales assistance, or deliver other enhancements. Here the trade-offs are real and binding.

Let's be clear. This is not to say that a value proposition built around low price cannot simultaneously offer some other dimensions of customer value. IKEA's design, one particular kind of quality, happens to be consistent with low costs as long as IKEA controls the costs of raw materials, manufacturing, and logistics. Southwest's convenience, another kind of quality, is also consistent with low costs. Frequent departures actually enhance Southwest's cost advantage, allowing for better utilization of planes and ground crews. And those convenient, frequent departures are themselves made possible by the many low-cost practices (no assigned seats, no baggage transfers) that allow Southwest to have fast gate turnarounds. Southwest cleverly stresses this type of quality, making a virtue of the trade-offs it has made. However, other dimensions of airline quality—an assigned seat, more legroom, a meal served on china—carry a real price tag.

When managers focus on execution, on making sure that they are "best practice" when it comes to generic activities, then *eliminating* trade-offs can be a good thing. When it comes to strategy, however, trade-offs are essential in making what you do unique. Finding trade-offs—IKEA's insight about the value of flat packs, for example—is essential to creating strategy. Maintaining and *steepening* trade-offs, making them even sharper, is essential to sustaining strategy.

network. Nonetheless, BA got caught on some of the same trade-offs as its American counterparts, muddling its premium reputation and confusing customers. Go's original advertising slogan was "the new low-cost airline from British Airways." Go selected airports closer to major cities than competitors like Ryanair, airports that were more crowded and more prone to delays. Also unlike most low-fare airlines, it gave passengers seat assignments and contracted food service to a high-end catering outfit.

After racking up somewhat-higher-than-expected losses, BA decided that running a low-cost airline was inconsistent with its positioning as a premium carrier. It sold Go to private equity firm 3i. Free from BA, Go launched an aggressive advertising campaign explicitly targeting BA customers. Only a year later, 3i was able to sell a larger Go to low-cost rival EasyJet at four times the price it had paid for the company.

Trade-offs make it tough for would-be straddlers. But straddling isn't the only way one company can copy another. Repositioning is another. When a company's existing position is no longer viable, it may try to reposition itself by copying someone else's strategy in its entirety. This is obviously hard to do—you have to build a new reputation and a new set of supporting activities and skills, and you also have to dismantle the old. Not surprising, repositioning of this sort is rare, as well it should be. A repositioner effectively chooses to run the same race as a rival who has a giant head start.

Home Improvement: Men Versus Women

Lowe's took a more strategic path when it recognized that it needed a new positioning. Home improvement retailing is a category made famous by the spectacular success of Home Depot in the 1980s and 1990s. Home Depot's original value proposition was this: it offered do-it-yourselfers, mainly men, the materials and the advice they needed to accomplish home improvements at low prices relative to the existing alternatives of hiring a contractor or buying from hardware stores. Home Depot offered the widest selection of items in huge, warehouse-style stores that averaged over 130,000 square feet. Its well-trained associates, many of whom were former trades people, provided advice and helped shoppers navigate the huge stores. The company appealed not only to do-it-yourselfers but also to smaller contractors. Both were attracted to Home Depot's merchandise assortment and low prices.

Home Depot's value proposition was so attractive, and its competitive advantage was so great, that many of the industry incumbents, typically regional chains with stores of between 20,000 and 30,000 square feet, were driven out of business. By 1988, Lowe's, then the largest do-it-yourself home improvement chain in the United States, could see the handwriting on the wall. Without a new strategy, it would become another casualty of Home Depot's success.

To address Home Depot's lower prices, Lowe's copied its larger store format. At the same time, however, Lowe's discovered a need that Home Depot wasn't meeting, which became the basis for a distinctive strategy. From surveying thousands of customers, Lowe's learned that women, not men, are the driving force for major home improvement projects, especially those involving design and fashion. That insight became the basis for Lowe's new value proposition.

Concentrating on women's needs gave rise to a number of trade-offs in product assortment and merchandising. Lowe's places greater emphasis on home fashion, kitchen, lawn and garden, decorating items, and consumer appliances—in line with its appeal to women. Lowe's aims to be price competitive with Home Depot on common items but to offer a higher proportion of unique and fashion items with better margins.

Trade-offs are choices that make strategies sustainable because they are not easy to match or to neutralize.

Instead of displaying piles of merchandise on palettes and racks, as Home Depot does, Lowe's created displays of kitchens, window treatments, and other items as they would appear in the home. This trade-off was less space efficient, but better suited to its target customers. Moving away from the warehouse ambience, Lowe's stores have lower ceilings, brighter lighting, and more attractive shelving. To keep its store format geared to its value proposition, Lowe's has made another important trade-off: it serves contractors through a separate division with separate and different facilities.

As a result of these decisions about assortment and the shopping experience, Lowe's stores must be restocked more frequently and in smaller quantities than Home Depot's—another important trade-off that has cost consequences. Each company has its own tailored approach to replenishing merchandise for its stores. The point is that Lowe's didn't try to copy everything from Home Depot. It carved out a different positioning, with a different value chain. Some customers and needs are better served by Lowe's. Some are better served by Home Depot. What makes both strategies robust are the many trade-offs required to carry them out. Lowe's achieves its competitive advantage through choices that are incompatible with Home Depot's, and vice versa.

In the early 2000s, Lowe's, starting from a smaller base, grew faster in sales and earnings. Some analysts were quick to proclaim Lowe's "the winner." For Porter, this was precisely the kind of destructive, zero-sum thinking that gets in the way of companies when they try to compete on uniqueness. Home Depot was having some performance problems at the time, but those were caused by poor store execution, not by poor strategy.

Lowe's was smart enough to copy the one element of Home Depot's success that had become vital for anyone in that industry, but it was also smart enough to stake out its own unique positioning. There was room for both companies to thrive, each pursuing its own path. Yet more recently, Home Depot has been copying Lowe's, adding, for example, a home décor line by Martha Stewart to appeal to women. Imitation that undermines key trade-offs—as this kind of move has the potential to do if carried too far—also undermines competitive advantage.

Choosing What *Not* to Do

Trade-offs make choices about what *not* to do as important as choices of what to do. Deciding which needs to serve and which products to offer is absolutely key to developing a strategy. But it is just as important to decide which needs you will not serve, and which products, features, or services you won't offer. And then comes the hard part—sticking to those decisions.

Companies tend over time to add functions and features to their products, hoping this will broaden their customer base and increase sales. The "more is better" psychology is hard to resist. The arguments that lead to feature creep are all too familiar: the incremental cost of adding a feature is minimal; we need the revenue growth; we have to match what our rivals are offering; our customers are telling us this is what they want. (For nonprofits, "mission creep"—off-target projects undertaken to please big donors or staff—is the analogous problem.)

This is the slippery slope that leads to competition to be the best. When you try to offer something for everyone, you tend to relax the trade-offs that underpin your competitive advantage. Wherever you find an organization that has sustained its competitive advantage over a period of many years, you can be sure that company has defended its key trade-offs against numerous onslaughts.

> When you try to offer something for everyone, you tend to relax the trade-offs that underpin your competitive advantage.

Often that onslaught takes the form of a new trend sweeping the industry. In the 1950s, a wave of new technology—microwaves, flash freezing, artificial flavorings—transformed the food industry. In-N-Out Burger, the purveyor of fresh food, freshly prepared, decided to take a pass on the latest food fads. As McDonald's and others switched to frozen beef patties, Harry Snyder (In-N-Out's founder) took the opposite fork in the road. He actually hired his own butcher to provide a reliable source of fresh beef.

In the late 1990s, nearly every brokerage firm rushed into online trading. No one wanted to be left behind. No one, that is, except Edward Jones, the retail brokerage we described in chapter 4. Edward Jones has built a distinct strategy around long-term relationships with conservative investors of modest means, a type of customer often ignored by the industry. We saw that Edward Jones built a dense network of retail offices because its chosen customer wants a face-to-face relationship with an individual, not an unfamiliar voice at a call center. Beyond personal attention, Jones understands that its particular customers value simple, conservative financial products combined with a steady, low-risk, buy-and-hold approach to investing.

During the boom years of the 1990s, there was intense industry and media pressure—and pressure from Jones's own brokers—to add Internet trading. The firm was criticized for being behind the times. But the management team (Jones is one of the last remaining partnerships in the industry) held its ground, having learned from Porter to appreciate the power of trade-offs. Internet trading, despite its media coronation as "the next big thing," was completely inconsistent with Jones's focus on face-to-face relationships and long-term investing.

Today, you can go to the Edward Jones Web site and you will find a tab with the title "When We Say No." It lays out what Edward Jones does *not* do: It doesn't serve high rollers and day traders. It doesn't sell derivatives, commodities, or penny stocks. It doesn't offer online trading because that "encourages rash decision making." It tells prospective clients it wants investors, not gamblers. Trade-offs like these are never easy. Make no mistake, Edward Jones has left money on the table. But at the same time, it has mastered what Porter calls one of the great paradoxes about trade-offs in competition. Executives often resist making trade-offs for fear they will lose some customers. The irony is that unless they make trade-offs and deliberately choose not to serve *all* customers and needs, then they are unlikely to do a good job of serving *any* customers and needs.

Clarity about what you won't do, then, is the best way to succeed at what you do choose to do. It is only by being deliberately unresponsive to some needs, by embracing strategic trade-offs, that companies can be genuinely responsive to other needs. Put another way, the role of trade-offs in strategy is deliberately to make some customers unhappy. Southwest Airlines tells a great story of how its legendary CEO, Herb Kelleher, dealt with a very frequent flyer they called the "Pen Pal" because she wrote so many complaint letters. First, think about the many trade-offs essential to Southwest's strategy. No assigned seats. No first class. No meals. No planes other than 737s. No baggage transfer. And so on. The Pen Pal complained about almost every choice Southwest makes. After sending numerous polite responses to her many letters, the customer relations people had run out of ideas. They asked Herb if he would reply. It didn't take him long to write the following:

"Dear Mrs. Crabapple, We will miss you. Love, Herb."

Herb Kelleher stories are often entertaining, but they are usually instructive as well. Building and sustaining competitive advantage means that you must be disciplined about saying no to a host of initiatives that would blur your uniqueness. The notion that the customer is always right is one of those half-truths that can lead to mediocre performance. Trade-offs explain why it is not true that you should give every customer what he or she wants. Some of those customers are not *your* customers, and you should send them packing, ideally with the same flair and humor that came naturally to Kelleher.

Or, as Porter puts it, "Strategy is making trade-offs in competing. The essence of strategy is choosing what not to do."

CHAPTER 6

Fit:

The Amplifier

THIS CHAPTER ADDRESSES THE fourth test of strategy, something Porter calls "fit." Fit has to do with how the activities in the value chain relate to one another. Its role in strategy highlights yet another popular misconception, that competitive success can be explained by one *core competence*, the one thing you do really well. The fallacy here is that good strategies don't rely on just *one* thing, on making *one* choice. Nor do they typically result from even a series of *independent* choices. Good strategies depend on the connection among *many* things, on making *interdependent* choices.

Good strategies depend on the connection
among *many* things, on making
interdependent choices.

We saw, in chapter 4, that a series of choices about a company's value proposition and its value chain gives rise to competitive advantage.

Where those choices involve trade-offs, the strategy becomes more valuable and more difficult to imitate (chapter 5). You can think of fit as an amplifier, raising the power of both of those effects. Fit amplifies the competitive advantage of a strategy by lowering costs or raising customer value (and price). Fit also makes a strategy more sustainable by raising barriers to imitation.

At one level, the idea of fit is completely intuitive. Every general manager knows the importance—and the difficulty—of aligning the various functional areas needed to compete in a business. Getting areas like marketing, production, service, and information technology (IT) all pulling in the same direction is usually easier said than done, especially in large organizations. But Porter has uncovered something even more substantial than alignment. Fit plays a larger and more complex role in competition than most realize.

What Is Fit?

In chapter 4 we explored how the activities a company performs relate to its value proposition. Here our focus is how those same activities relate to each other. Let's look at just a dozen of IKEA's many tailored activity choices:

1. Network of product designers (controlled product development)

2. Centrally managed global supply chain (outsourced manufacturing)

3. Huge stores

4. Warehouse attached to stores (the last stop in the store layout)

5. Suburban locations with easy highway access

6. Ample free parking

7. No sales associates on the showroom floor

8. Fully decorated full-room product displays

9. Large informational hang-tags on every item (with price, dimensions, materials)

10. Items in flat packs (product assembly and delivery "outsourced" to customers)

11. In-store cafeterias

12. In-store childcare/playroom

Flat packs, as we saw in chapter 5, play a big role in IKEA's competitive advantage because they lower the costs of shipping and product damage. So as an independent choice, flat packs support IKEA's low-price positioning. Suburban store locations lower costs because land is cheaper outside the city limits. But these two choices are, of course, interdependent. The value of those flat packs is amplified by the car-friendly locations that make it easier for customers to load their purchases into their cars.

Go down the list of activities and you will see many such examples of fit. Huge stores amplify the value of global-scale product sourcing. Huge stores are more valuable if customers are willing to spend more time per visit. The free childcare and the in-house cafeteria make it possible (and even enjoyable, if you like Swedish meatballs) for customers to take their time. Each of these choices enhances the value of the others. All contribute to lower prices for customers. The huge store format gives IKEA space to showcase all its merchandise in fully decorated room displays. These, along with the large product information hang-tags, allow IKEA to do without sales associates—another cost saving that arises because one activity impacts the value of another. That, in fact, is a good working definition: *fit means that the value or cost of one activity is affected by the way other activities are performed.*

Fit means that the value or cost of one activity is affected by the way other activities are performed.

You need a car to benefit from IKEA's value system. In contrast, if you shop at the fashion retailer Zara, you probably arrive on foot. Zara is part of the Spanish group Inditex (Industria de Diseño Textil, S.A.), the world's largest clothing retailer by revenue. Zara's stores are prominently located in urban centers with heavy foot traffic. It has built such a hot fashion brand that most French women think this Spanish company must be French.

Zara sells the latest-fashion clothes at moderate prices (not low in absolute terms, but low relative to fashion brands). Its key insight into how to deliver that particular value proposition is speed. Everything Zara does is tailored to getting the latest styles into its stores fast. Most fashion retailers can live with lead times of three months. Zara's are just two to four weeks, allowing it to release one hundred collections per year.

This blistering pace is possible because Zara controls its value chain from end to end, and its choices all along the value chain are different from its rivals. Zara makes some significant trade-offs—in how it promotes its brand, how it designs its merchandise, and how it manages production, logistics, and inventory. Zara's success comes not from one choice, but from the way these many choices fit together to reinforce each other.

Think of Zara as a system perfectly designed to optimize the delivery of its distinctive value proposition. I say "optimize" because if you look at what Zara does, piece by piece, some of the choices will surprise you. Some of its choices, for example, may not seem cost effective given Zara's low relative price positioning. Its large design team is twice the size of H&M's, another hot European fashion retailer. Unlike its rivals, Zara does its own manufacturing, and most of it is done in Europe, not Asia. Its stores are located in the highest-rent districts in town. None of these choices is, by itself, the "low cost" solution. But when you step back and look at the whole, as a system, you realize that Zara is willing to make a suboptimal choice in one area in order to optimize the whole.

So how does Zara do it? Let's see how the pieces of this puzzle all fit together. First, the role of the designers is to spot trends and copy them. Rather than pay big-name designers big bucks to create something new, the company has scouts around the world looking for the latest fashion trends at shows and in nightclubs. Its large team of in-house designers can create a new collection in under a month and can modify existing collections in a couple of weeks. The size of the team allows Zara to be a fast copier, getting those new designs into production quickly.

Zara began not as a retailer but as a manufacturer, and true to its roots it continues to do a sizeable amount of production in-house, in Europe, and in plants configured for small-batch production. Zara owns a fleet of trucks to speed goods from its centralized logistics hubs in Spain to its stores throughout Europe in twenty-four hours or less. And, again counter to industry practice, garments arrive ticketed and hung. This raises shipping costs but means the merchandise arrives ready to sell, needing no in-store ironing. Speed is the theme.

The stores themselves—in prominent locations with high foot traffic—are spacious. But the new goods that come twice a week arrive in limited supply, sending a clear message: buy it now or lose the opportunity. Store personnel provide constant feedback about what's selling and what isn't, information that helps Zara make better real-time decisions about design and production volumes.

Now think about the customer experience: the steady flow of new merchandise combined with eye-catching stores that serve as billboards for the store combined with a scarcity of goods. This generates buzz. Customers talk about Zara with their friends. They keep coming back because they know the selection will be different, and they can see the changing merchandise as they walk past the stores.

All of this adds up to produce Zara's superior results, its competitive advantage. Where in Zara's financials do you see that advantage? Here's one example. Zara's customers shop more often than customers of comparable stores, and they buy more merchandise at full price. According to data I saw a few years ago, Zara was marking down about 10 percent of items versus the industry average of 17 to 20 percent. In retailing, that's a huge advantage. And Zara's markdown advantage is not the result of one choice. It is not simply that its merchandisers make smarter buying decisions, for example. It is the result of many choices that make up Zara's "system."

Here's another example of how Zara's advantage hits its P&L. Most fashion brands are built and supported by a substantial advertising budget (ad spending for the category averages about 3 to 4 percent of sales). Ad spending at H&M has been about 5 percent. In contrast, a general merchandise retailer such as Walmart spends less than one-third of one percent of its revenue on advertising. But once you think about the implications of the fit across Zara's activity choices, you won't be surprised to learn that Zara's ad spending has been right down there at Walmart's level. Zara spends more on store locations, but almost nothing on advertising. Its many choices combine to generate customer enthusiasm without the aid of heavy spending on marketing.

How Fit Works

Fit can take a number of forms, although the distinctions among them are often blurred in practice. Each of the three types Porter identifies works in a slightly different way to affect competitive advantage.

The first kind of fit is basic consistency, where each activity is aligned with the company's value proposition and each contributes incrementally to its dominant themes. Think about the speed that is critical to Zara's success. At every step in the value chain, Zara has configured its activities so that nothing takes longer than it needs to: its design teams are configured for rapid response; its plants are located nearby; its own fleet of trucks ensures rapid delivery; its investments in IT speed communications between design and manufacturing. Each activity contributes to Zara's speed. Zara passes the basic consistency test.

When activities are inconsistent, they cancel each other out. A client of mine wanted to position itself to be a low-cost provider of socks to the leading discounters. At the same time that its plant managers were trying to cut costs, sales was allowing—even encouraging—its retail customers of all sizes to order one-of-a-kind colors that required customized production. These "one-of-a-kind colors" weren't what you'd think. For example, there were literally hundreds of variations on the color white, each requiring a unique dye formula. The plant had to produce in batches larger than the customers' order quantities. The result was so much excess inventory that, laid end to end, the socks would have circled the globe. (Here's an example where "the numbers" jolted the company into action.) This wasn't the first company, nor will it be the last, to struggle with the alignment between sales and manufacturing. Expressed mathematically, consistency means that $1 + 1 + 1 = 3$, and not some number *less* than 3. Inconsistent activities make the whole *less* than the sum of the parts.

A second type of fit occurs when activities complement or reinforce each other. This is real synergy, where the value of each activity is raised by the other. Zara's high-traffic store locations and the large number of collections reinforce each other. The high-visibility locations help Zara with its goal of turning over all of a store's merchandise every two weeks. Large display windows are like a beacon drawing customers in.

Or consider that Netflix offers its members access to an enormous library of films (initially by holding inventory of DVDs at regional warehouses; increasingly through digital distribution). It also maintains a thriving, user-generated movie-rating system that by 2010 had produced over a billion ratings. "The real problem we're trying to solve," explains CEO Reed Hastings, "is how do you transform movie selection so that consumers can find a steady stream of movies they love? It's a huge matching problem. We've got 55,000 DVD titles over here. There are 300 million Americans over there. But most people can't tell you ten movies they're dying to see." The ratings and the huge library are complementary: the reviews help members to broaden their movie-watching tastes, thereby making the large film library more valuable.

Home Depot provides another example of how activities reinforce each other. The basic Home Depot value proposition has three legs: huge selection, everyday low prices, and knowledgeable service. Nobody before had put these all together. The large warehouse store format was essential to offering both selection and low prices. But without excellent service, customers would have felt lost in the warehouse stores.

In the late 1970s, founders Bernie Marcus and Arthur Blank hired knowledgeable employees—at the time a radical notion—paid them well, and cultivated a religion of customer service. When customers asked where they could find a given item, for example, Home Depot employees were trained to walk with the customer to the correct aisle. Marcus is reputed to have told his employees that if he caught them pointing instead of accompanying the customer, he would "rip their finger off." Store size and service reinforced each other at Home Depot. Without the service, the size would not have worked.

It's interesting to compare and contrast Home Depot with IKEA. Both used large-format stores to support a low-price positioning, but while Home Depot's positioning and product variety made personal service a necessity, IKEA's made it irrelevant. In each case, the trade-offs and the fit across the value chain are strategy specific.

Porter's third type of fit is substitution. Here performing one activity makes it possible to eliminate another. IKEA's full-room displays and product hang-tags substitute for sales associates. Zara's prominent store locations and the rapid turnover of its collections make traditional advertising unnecessary. Increasingly, companies have learned to cooperate with suppliers or customers or both in order to optimize efforts across company boundaries. For its large business customers, for example, Dell will load customized software onto new PCs. Dell can do this faster and cheaper during the assembly process than a customer's IT department, which would have to load the software machine by machine after the PCs have been delivered. This substitution lowers the total cost, allowing Dell to share some of the savings with its customers. Substitution, then, works to optimize a company's value chain.

All three types of fit are common, and they often overlap. In companies with good strategies, fit tends to be both pervasive and complex.

Fit and Core Competence

Fit, as Porter conceives of it, sheds new light on a fundamental question of strategy: Where does competitive advantage come from? In

Mapping Your Activity System

Porter has created a tool he calls an "activity system map" to chart a company's significant activities, their relationship to the value proposition, and to each other.

You can start by identifying the core elements of the value proposition. For IKEA, I would highlight three: distinctive design, low prices, and immediate use.

You then identify the most salient activities performed in the business, those most responsible for creating customer value or those that generate significant cost. Try to list the unique activity choices at each step. This makes contrasts between the company and its competitors more obvious. For instance, even a cursory glance at IKEA's value chain compared with that of a traditional furniture store would highlight its unique configuration of in-store service and delivery.

Next, place activities on the map as shown in the following figure. Draw lines wherever there is fit—where an activity contributes to the value proposition and where two activities affect each other. On the IKEA map, flat packs contribute to low prices and immediate use. They affect self-delivery by customers. And so on. Were you to fully map IKEA's activities, you'd end up with an extremely dense and tangled web. For strategy, this is a good thing. Conversely, a map with sparse connections likely signals that the strategy is weak.

An activity map can help you see how well each activity supports the overall positioning—the customers served, the needs met, the relative price. For each activity, ask how it could be better linked to the overall strategy, even activities such as order processing or logistics that might seem to be largely generic in character. In most

IKEA's activity map

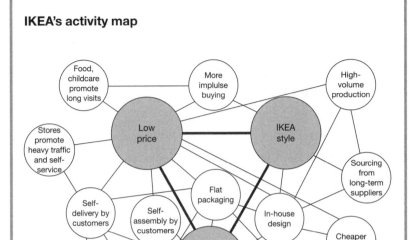

organizations, Porter observes, there are activities whose alignment has been ignored because they were not seen as part of strategy.

An activity map can help you identify ways to strengthen fit. Managers responsible for each activity can usually tell you whether their performance is impaired by other activities. They may also have ideas about how to improve the fit across activities. Look beyond basic consistency. Can you find new ways in which activities can reinforce each other or where one activity can substitute for others?

An activity map might also spur creativity about how to make a strategy more sustainable. Can you find new activities, or enhancements to what you already do, whose cost or effectiveness is improved by your *existing activity system*? Are there services, features, or product varieties that you can offer (and rivals cannot) because of the other things that you already do? Extensions like these will be the hardest for rivals to imitate.

many companies, the search for competitive advantage focuses on what are variously called critical resources, core capabilities, or key success factors. Although there are technical differences among these terms, managers generally use them interchangeably and lump them together under the umbrella term *core competence*. All reflect a similar point of view: that competitive advantage comes from a small number of factors, be they intangible skills or hard assets. The way to compete, then, is to acquire and develop those core competences.

A common mistake in strategy is to choose the same core competences as everyone else in your industry. If, for example, you believe that only a few things matter to competition, then you will race to acquire those valuable things before your rivals do. Entire industries have rushed headlong to control a "strategic" resource—for example, an installed base of customers (e.g., cellular subscribers), distribution channels (e.g., television stations or cable systems, stock brokers), or product portfolios (e.g., film libraries)—driving up the costs of those resources. In this vein, AT&T acquired the cable companies TCI, MediaOne, and part of Cablevision for $130 billion in 1999–2000. Just two years later, these assets were sold to Comcast for $44 billion. Oops. It is not hard to see where this approach to competition leads: imitation, competitive convergence, zero-sum competition to be the best.

A common mistake in strategy is to choose
the same core competences as everyone else
in your industry.

Fit means that the whole matters more than any individual part, that many things together create value, not just a few things in isolation. What, for example, accounts for Zara's success? Is it Zara's flair

Keep the Core, Outsource the Rest? Not So Fast

What is your core competence? And if that's the question you are asking about your own organization, aren't you less likely to be paying attention to tailoring, trade-offs, and fit? If just a few things matter in competition, then many things don't matter at all. The logic of core competences has led many companies to pursue outsourcing without thinking through the strategic consequences. The standard argument has been that companies should focus on their core activities. Those that aren't "core" can be outsourced to more efficient providers.

But once you appreciate the role of fit, you will stop and think much harder about outsourcing. Instead of trying to determine which activities are *core*, Porter asks a different question: Which activities are *generic* and which are *tailored*? Generic activities—those that cannot be meaningfully tailored to a company's position—can be safely outsourced to more efficient external suppliers. However, Porter argues that outsourcing is risky for activities that are or could be tailored to strategy, and especially for those activities that are strongly complementary with others. The fewer elements that remain in the company's value chain, the fewer the opportunities to extend tailoring, trade-offs, and fit.

The initial outsourcing decision almost always results in short-term cost savings, but the longer-term implications for both cost and competitive convergence are troubling. Outsourcing can not only limit the opportunities for uniqueness and fit in the company's strategy but also push an entire industry into greater homogenization.

for fashion? Its flexible European manufacturing? Its store locations? Its approach to logistics? The answer isn't to be found in one or two core competences. The answer lies in the fit among all of Zara's value-creating activities. Zara's strategy involves a series of choices made simultaneously. Zara's success depends on a whole system of interdependent activities, not just one or two powerful parts. It comes not only from the trade-offs Zara has made in configuring its activities but also from the way those activities impact each other.

Fit means that the competitive value of individual activities—and the associated skills, competences, or resources—cannot be decoupled from the system or the strategy. Whether it is Southwest or Zara, Home Depot or Lowe's, Enterprise or Zipcar, In-N-Out Burger or McDonald's, Edward Jones or Netflix, value comes not from "core competences" alone, but from how they are deployed in the company's positioning.

Fit Makes Strategy More Sustainable

Fit not only amplifies competitive advantage by enhancing value or lowering costs, but also makes that advantage more sustainable. We saw in chapter 5 that trade-offs make it hard for rivals to copy a successful strategy. Fit makes it even harder. To get the benefit of imitation, you now have to copy a whole nest of interdependent activities.

Porter argues that fit deters imitation in a number of ways. First, rivals will have a hard time figuring out what they have to match. If you wanted to copy Zara, what exactly would you copy? Its approach to product design? The store configurations? Its manufacturing operations? Its fleet of trucks? Basic consistency may be readily discerned by rivals, but the more a company's positioning rests on complex fit, the harder it is for rivals to know exactly what it is they are trying to copy. Unless you're an insider, it's very difficult to untangle what's going on.

Second, even if rivals can identify the relevant interconnections, they will have a hard time replicating all of them because fit is organizationally challenging. It's one thing to copy product features or a particular sales-force approach. It's another to match a whole system of activities, something that typically requires the integration of decisions and actions across work groups, departments, and functions.

By throwing multiple obstacles in the path of would-be imitators, fit lowers the odds that a strategy can be copied. To make this concrete, Porter uses a simple mathematical argument. Let's assume you have a 90 percent probability of matching any one activity. If you then have to match a system with two activities, your probability of success is 81 percent (0.9×0.9). If there are four activities, your probability of success drops to 66 percent ($0.9 \times 0.9 \times 0.9 \times 0.9$). And so on.

> By throwing multiple obstacles in the path of would-be imitators, fit lowers the odds that a strategy can be copied.

Now think about how likely it is that someone can successfully copy IKEA or Zara. Once you see strategy as a system of interconnected choices (figure 6-1), you can grasp how quickly the probabilities compound to make a good strategy sustainable. Moreover, as fit lowers the probability of successful imitation, it raises the penalty for failure precisely because the activities are interconnected. A small shortfall in one can produce ripple effects elsewhere, as we saw with British Airway's failed low-cost carrier, Go.

There is a subtle corollary to this last point. Porter observes that companies with strong fit are typically superior in both strategy *and* execution, and thus they are less likely to attract imitators in the first place. Why? When activities affect each other, flaws in one will impair overall performance. This tends to shine a spotlight on weaknesses, making it more likely they will be addressed. It also means there is more upside in addressing operational shortfalls, and often more pressure to do so. The resulting strength of companies like these is another deterrent to imitation.

In chapter 4 we saw that a tailored value chain—*different activities*—was the first line of defense against imitation. In chapter 5, we saw that trade-offs constitute a second line of defense. Tailoring and trade-offs prevent *existing* rivals from copying a good strategy, either by straddling or repositioning. The more activities rivals have to reconfigure, the more damage they will do to their current positions.

FIGURE 6-1

Zara's interconnected choices

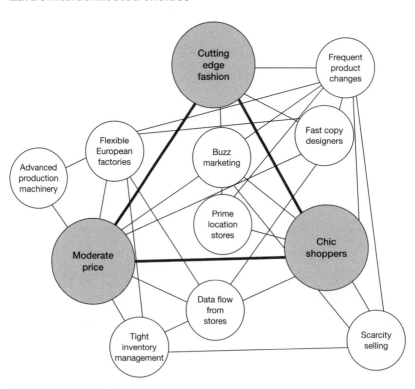

Finally, fit explains how competitive advantage can be sustained against new entrants, even the most determined of them. In competing to be the best, imitation is easy, and advantages are temporary. The more a company competes on uniqueness, the less susceptible it is to imitation, and advantages can be sustained over long periods of time. Great strategies are like complex systems in which all of the parts fit together seamlessly. Each thing you do amplifies the value of the other things you do. That enhances competitive advantage. And it enhances sustainability as well. "Fit," Porter says, "locks out imitators by creating a chain that is as strong as its strongest link."

CHAPTER 7

Continuity:

The Enabler

W E COME NOW TO the fifth and final test of strategy: continuity over time. To recap: the first two tests—a unique value proposition and a tailored value chain—are the core of a strategy. Trade-offs, the third test, are the economic linchpin. They make differences in price and cost possible and sustainable. Fit, the fourth test, is an amplifier, enhancing the cost and price differences that are the essence of competitive advantage, and making it even harder for rivals to copy the strategy. Continuity is the enabler. All the other elements of strategy—tailoring, trade-offs, fit—take time to develop. Without continuity, organizations are unlikely to develop competitive advantage in the first place.

This generation of business leaders has been preoccupied with change. It has been flooded with advice about how to deal with the accelerating pace of change, how to overcome resistance to change, how to lead large-scale change efforts, and so on. A lot of the change literature aimed at managers is motivational. It's about firing up the organization. But it has produced an overheated rhetoric that can

FIGURE 7-1

The five tests of a good strategy

1. A UNIQUE VALUE PROPOSITION

Are you offering distinctive value to a chosen set of customers at the right relative price?

2. A TAILORED VALUE CHAIN

Is the best set of activities to deliver *your* value proposition *different from* the activities performed by rivals?

3. TRADE-OFFS DIFFERENT FROM RIVALS

Are you clear about what you *won't* do so that you can deliver *your* kind of value most efficiently and effectively?

4. FIT ACROSS THE VALUE CHAIN

Is the value of your activities enhanced by the other activities you perform?

5. CONTINUITY OVER TIME

Is there enough stability in the core of your strategy to allow your organization to get good at what it does, to foster tailoring, trade-offs, and fit?

---

undermine good strategy. Now, every change is referred to as "disruptive," no matter how slow or sudden, how shallow or deep its impact might be. Think about how often you hear the phrases "constant reinvention" and "radical transformation."

Yes, competition is dynamic, not static, and the arena in which companies operate is constantly changing. Customers' needs shift. New competitors emerge. Old technologies evolve and new ones are created. Dealing with change is an essential part of strategy. Everyone can come up with examples of once-proud companies brought low either by their failure to see the need for change or to execute it effectively.

But continuity, as pedestrian as it sounds, is also essential. Whereas the spotlight is more often directed at companies that change too little, Porter highlights an equal, if not greater, mistake: companies can change too much, and in the wrong ways. And, he argues, having a strategy—making choices, defining limits—doesn't impair your ability to change. It actually facilitates the right kind of innovation.

Why Is Continuity Essential?

As we've seen, strategy involves all aspects of an organization's approach to the market. It is inherently complex. Think about what it takes to understand and serve your customers, to create real value for them. Think about the links between your organization and its suppliers and its partners. Think about the hundreds of activities you perform, and how these must be aligned with your value proposition and with each other. And then remember that all of this involves engaging and aligning the actions of hundreds or even hundreds of thousands of individuals who do the work.

Allow me one cooking metaphor: strategy isn't a stir fry; it's a stew. It takes time for the flavors and textures to develop. Over time, as all of a company's constituents—internal and external—come to a deeper understanding of what a company can offer them, or what they can offer to it, a whole raft of activities become better tailored to the strategy and better aligned with each other. This aspect of strategy is very fundamentally about people and their capacity to absorb and process change. Consider how continuity enables competitive advantage:

- Continuity reinforces a company's identity—it builds a company's brand, its reputation, and its customer relationships. This principle is well understood at In-N-Out Burger, an outlier in today's hyperactive, hipper-than-thou business culture. The company is proud of its old-fashioned menu (fresh beef, real potatoes, real ice cream in the shakes) and its old-fashioned values (treat employees like family). Its fanatically loyal customers brag about how far they're willing to drive for their In-N-Out fix, or how long they'll wait in line when a new location opens. The company Web site strikes exactly the right note: "Though times have changed, little has changed at In-N-Out." You'll find today exactly what "customers have enjoyed since 1948."

There has been far more change at BMW or IKEA or Disney, but customers will never mistake what these companies stand for, what needs they can and cannot meet. In other words, they understand the core value proposition and the major trade-offs. A good strategy, consistently maintained over time through repeated interactions with customers, is what gives power to a brand.

- **Continuity helps suppliers, channels, and other outside parties to contribute to a company's competitive advantage.** This is all about alignment and tailoring. Continuity of strategy, for example, allowed Dell in the 1990s and early 2000s to establish productive relationships with key suppliers that could better adapt to its needs. Austin, Texas, became home to hundreds of suppliers encouraged by Dell to co-locate warehouses and production nearby. The resulting cluster of related companies included manufacturers of semiconductors and electronics, software companies, and technology consulting and services firms. (*Clusters* play a special role in competition. See the glossary for more on this.) The longer outside parties work with a company, the better they understand its goals and methods.

The benefits can flow both ways. Continuity has enabled the Swiss food giant Nestlé to develop a thriving supply base of local farmers for its milk business in India. Starting in the 1960s with just 180 farmers, Nestlé built refrigerated dairies as collection points for milk. Over time it provided technical assistance, training, and supplies to the farmers, who have become vastly more productive (and prosperous) as a result. The number of farmers working with Nestlé has grown to over 75,000.

Continuity of strategy produces similar benefits in the labor market, another source of supply, allowing companies such as Enterprise and Southwest Airlines to attract employees who fit the company's strategy. It also fosters relationships with distribution channels, which take time to develop. When Toyota launched its premium auto, the Lexus, it invested heavily, and over many years, to create its dealer network. If Toyota weren't committed to this strategy for the long term, the investment would not have made much sense.

- Continuity fosters improvements in individual activities and fit across activities; it allows an organization to build unique capabilities and skills tailored to its strategy. The continuity of strategy at Aravind Eye Hospital, for example, allowed it to develop customized training programs for its own staff, as well as courses to increase the supply of skilled eye care providers for India at large. Today Aravind's "curriculum" is extensive, ranging from residency programs for ophthalmologists to nonclinical courses for technicians in instrument maintenance. Or consider Southwest Airlines and Four Seasons Hotels, two companies distinguished by their unique styles of service. Over many years, each has honed its hiring practices. Each can screen more effectively for employees with the skills and attitudes that fit the company's strategy. It is in this way that consistent pursuit of a strategy over time allows a company to develop a whole raft of strategy-specific assets—including its culture—that become hard to match.

Continuity increases the odds that people throughout the organization will understand the company's strategy and how they can contribute to it. The more they "get it," the more likely they are to make decisions that reinforce and extend the strategy. Managers will be more likely to align activities that had been working at cross-purposes. The point to underscore here is that skill development and alignment rarely happen overnight.

For the very same reasons that continuity is valuable, companies pay a high price for frequent shifts in strategy. These require reconfiguration of activities and realigning entire systems. Customers and value chain partners have to be reeducated about what the company is now trying to do, which typically means heavy reinvestments in brand and image. To cite one example, Sears, beginning in the 1980s, jumped from one *strategy du jour* to another, confusing its customers about what the company stood for. Known for many years as a seller of tools and appliances, it tried to become, first, a financial services provider, then a fashion retailer, and then a one-stop shopping experience under the implausible slogan "From Stocks to Socks." Sears lurched from one initiative to another, from "The Store of the Future" to "Everyday Low Pricing" to "Brand Central" to "The Softer Side of Sears" and "The Great Indoors." As one Sears manager put it, "We got good ideas from corporate . . . Each idea would come, falter, and go, and in six months there would be another idea. After a while we stopped believing in the ideas."

It usually takes years, not months, to successfully implement a new strategy. Think about "One Ford," the name given to Ford Motor Company's repositioning under CEO Alan Mulally. Ford had been floundering for decades by the time it hired him from Boeing in 2006.

Mulally dropped the "house of brands" assembled by his predecessors, selling off Jaguar, Land Rover, Aston Martin, and Volvo. Focusing on the Ford badge, Mulally is shifting the emphasis from trucks and SUVs to smaller, more environmentally friendly passenger cars. He is also betting that the needs and tastes of customers around the globe are converging—that it will make less and less sense to design cars specifically for one market or another. The 2012 Focus is the company's first truly global car.

Now think about what a strategy shift like this involves for a company with 200,000 employees. Old ways of doing things had to be dismantled and unlearned as new structures, systems, and processes were put in place. Product development had to be overhauled. Production capacity had to be reduced. Labor agreements had to be renegotiated. Marketing needed to be revamped. Four years into the process, Mulally estimates it will take another three years for 80 percent of Ford's products to be built on global platforms.

The managerial challenge is enormous. Recall Porter's simple mathematical explanation of why copying a strategy is likely to produce less-than-stellar results: when the probabilities of getting each activity right are less than 1, the probability of getting four or five things right quickly deteriorates ($0.9 \times 0.9 \times 0.9 \times 0.9 \times 0.9 = 0.59$). The same logic explains why frequent shifts in strategy are likely to be a significant drag on performance. Some activities, practices, skills, or attitudes will never catch up with the new strategy.

What Does Continuity Involve?

Continuity of strategy does not mean that an organization should stand still. As long as there is stability in the core value proposition, there can, and should, be enormous innovation in how it's delivered. In fact, successful companies rarely have to reinvent themselves because they are constantly reinventing their methods. They keep getting better at what they do. They keep searching for ways to create more value, to make the pie bigger.

Continuity of strategy does not mean that an organization should stand still. As long as there is stability in the core value proposition, there can, and should, be enormous innovation in how it's delivered.

In 1850, Paul Julius Reuter found an ingenious way to speed the delivery of global financial information to market participants. His new technology was the carrier pigeon. The company Reuter founded survives to this day, although the pigeons gave way to a series of technological innovations, beginning with the telegraph and culminating in the Internet. Reuters continues to serve the enduring need for rapid information about financial markets, albeit with a very different set of activities today than it used more than 150 years ago.

Look at India's Aravind Eye Hospital today and you will see a large, complex organization that offers a full range of eye care services. It partners with local community leaders and service groups to run free screening eye camps, an outreach mechanism that brings care and education to over 2.3 million patients a year in rural villages. In 1992, as Aravind's volume of surgeries had grown to scale, it backward integrated into the production of lenses, one of its most expensive supplies. Its manufacturing division, Aurolab, makes intraocular lenses, as well as other consumables used in eye surgery. From its very humble origins in 1976, starting with three doctors and eleven beds, there have been vast changes in both Aravind's scale and scope, but it continues to serve the enduring need for affordable eye care.

A Walmart store today looks very different from its counterpart of 1962, the year the discount retailer was founded. Walmart's first stores served customers in small-town, rural America, markets that were not served by other discounters. Walmart now operates in markets of all sizes, all around the globe. It is a leader in categories that Sam Walton never dreamed of selling. Today, for example, Walmart is the largest seller of groceries in the United States, a business that Walmart entered only in the late 1980s. It sells more DVDs than any other retailer, a category Walmart entered in 1999. Despite five decades of dramatic change in the merchandise it sells, modifications in its store formats and systems, and continuous improvements in productivity, the basic value proposition is unchanged: Walmart continues to offer its customers branded merchandise at everyday low prices.

In each of these cases, change has been enabled by continuity of direction. That's where stability is most important—in the basic value proposition, the core of needs the company meets and its relative price.

Continuity Under Uncertainty

One of the most difficult facts of life for managers is having to make decisions under conditions of uncertainty. And if you operate in a highly uncertain environment, it's easy to get caught in a false syllogism that goes something like this:

I can't predict the future.

Strategy requires a prediction of the future.

Therefore, I can't commit to a strategy.

If you can't predict what's going to happen next quarter, let alone three to five years from now, maybe it's safer to stay flexible, run harder, and sleep faster. This logic has pervaded the debate about competition for at least the past decade, if not longer.

But the second premise, Porter argues, is flawed. Great strategies are rarely, if ever, built on a particularly detailed or concrete prediction of the future. Walmart, for example, found itself in the midst of a revolution in retailing, yet its strategy didn't require Walmart to predict the direction that revolution would take. Since In-N-Out Burger's launch in 1948, there has been nothing short of a revolution in the way food is produced, prepared, and consumed, yet its strategy didn't depend on its ability to predict any of those massive changes. BMW's strategy didn't require unusual foresight about events that have shaken the auto industry, ranging from an oil shock to the emergence of China as the world's fastest-growing car market.

Great strategies are rarely, if ever, built on a particularly detailed or concrete prediction of the future.

You need only a very broad sense of which customers and needs are going to be relatively robust five or ten years from now. Strategy is implicitly a bet that the chosen customers or needs—and the essential trade-offs for meeting them at the right price—will be enduring.

In that sense, some value propositions turn out to be more robust than others. Dell's direct business model was based on the fact that some customers didn't want, or didn't need, a retailer or an intermediary such as a reseller to give them advice and information. The brilliance of that positioning choice in the early years of personal computers was that, as customers became more comfortable with computers, the number of customers willing to forego an intermediary would probably grow, not shrink. Dell was positioned in a strategy that was likely to have more growth opportunity than other strategies. In that sense, Dell made an implicit forecast that proved to be correct, at least up until a few years ago (see "When Does Strategy Need to Change?").

The strategy of America Online (AOL) was the mirror image of Dell's. AOL helped to introduce millions of people to the Internet, making the experience user friendly and charging a premium price for doing so. This positioning choice had an inherent vulnerability. As customers grew more comfortable going online, they would be less likely to need what AOL was configured to deliver. They would inevitably trade up from simple Web pages and hand-holding to deeper functionality or faster speed. Or they would trade down to a more stripped-down Internet service provider at a lower price.

Beyond this fundamental bet that the chosen needs will be enduring, strategy does not require what Porter calls "heroic predictions" about the future. Southwest Airlines had only to predict that people would continue to want low-cost, convenient transportation. They did not have to predict the rising concern over terrorism, or the price of jet fuel, or any of a host of variables that have had an impact on the airline industry. In-N-Out Burger had only to predict that some people would continue to want simple fresh burgers and fries, freshly prepared. Similarly, BMW had only to predict that the need for design, driving performance, and prestige would be enduring.

Alan Mulally is building Ford's future around a simple prediction that consumers across the globe are becoming more similar in what they want from a car. The strategy doesn't depend on how steep the penetration curve will be for electric vehicles, although that could potentially be a blockbuster technological disruption—if it happens at all. Says Mulally, "'That is what strategy is all about. It's about a point of view about the future and then making decisions based on that. The worst thing you can do is not have a point of view, and not make decisions.'" Porter couldn't have said it better himself.

When Does Strategy Need to Change?

The longer a strategy has been successful, the more difficult it may be to see genuine threats that might invalidate it. Continuity does not mean complacency, but, people being human, complacency can set in if managers aren't vigilant. Good strategies have staying power, but there are clearly times when a strategy must be changed. In Porter's view, these so-called inflection points are relatively rare, and companies are more likely to pull away from their strategies prematurely. It is therefore important to understand the conditions that absolutely require new strategies.

First, as customer needs change, a company's core value proposition may simply become obsolete. Often, as needs shift, companies are able to evolve to serve them, but not always. The real problem occurs when the needs disappear.

Founded in 1976, Liz Claiborne met an emerging need for a generation of women entering the professional workforce for the first time. Liz Claiborne gave its customers the security that they would be dressed appropriately for success. Tapping into this new need, Liz Claiborne grew rapidly and profitably. Throughout the 1980s, the company was a stellar performer. By the early 1990s, however, women's fashion insecurity in the workplace had diminished. After a decade of relying on Liz Claiborne for fashion guidance, women became more confident about their own choices and more interested in variety. At the same time, office dress codes loosened up. The need Liz Claiborne served so well shrank rapidly. Earnings dropped from $223 million in 1991 to $83 million in 1994.

Many factors beyond demographics and social change can cause customer needs to shift. Significant changes in regulation, for example, typically alter the mix of buyer value and cost that companies can offer. Regulation can hold an industry in an artificial equilibrium by defining customer needs in an arbitrary way. Deregulation can unleash pent-up economic forces, allowing new needs to emerge. Major structural changes in an industry often require new strategic positions.

Second, innovation of all sorts can serve to invalidate the essential trade-offs on which a strategy relies. Dell's strategy, meeting basic PC needs at low relative prices, was based on the cost advantages of its direct model. That strategy worked for the better part of two decades. But the rise of Taiwanese ODMs (original design manufacturers) has enabled rivals like Hewlett-Packard to outsource design and assembly, basically wiping out Dell's cost advantage. Dell has also struggled with the shift in PC sales from large business customers to consumers and with the sharp rise in the percentage of industry sales sold through the retail channel. These changes neutralized Dell's most important trade-offs. When I interviewed Michael Dell in the late 1990s, he said he worried about people at Dell "who talk about 'the model' as if it were an all-powerful being that will take care of everything. It's scary because I know that nothing is ever 100 percent constant." His concern turned out to be prophetic. A company needs a new strategy if its value chain does not allow it to outperform its competitors in delivering its unique value proposition.

Third, a technological or managerial breakthrough can completely trump a company's existing value proposition. Of all the forces that threaten strategies, none gets more attention than technology. Sometimes new technology changes the rules of the game; often it does not. A truly disruptive technology will invalidate the assets of the current generation of industry leaders. Digital photography was a disruptive technology for Kodak, the dominant producer of photographic film. For most uses, digital photography is superior to film. As a result, the value of Kodak's existing chemistry-based assets, assembled over a 100-year history, has been decimated. But even in this extreme case, in which Kodak will have to invest billions to assemble new expertise in electronics, the company still has its valuable brand and other assets on which to build a new future.

To determine whether a technology is truly disruptive, ask whether it can be integrated into the company's existing value chain or customized in a way that enhances the company's existing activities. In practice, Porter argues, truly disruptive technologies are quite rare.

Go back to the false syllogism we started with. Many executives, cheered on by management gurus, have embraced flexibility as an alternative to strategy. But if you apply the economic fundamentals of competitive advantage, you'll be quick to spot the flaw in this approach. Ask yourself, Where's the link between flexibility and superior performance? Is it likely that flexibility will meet any customer's needs better than a strategy sharply focused on those needs? Will hedging your activities—going halfway, doing some, not all—likely result in higher prices and lower costs? The problem, Porter argues, is that when you *substitute* flexibility for strategy, your organization never stands for anything or becomes good at anything. Flexibility sounds good in theory, but trace it down to the concrete level of the activities you perform and you'll see why flexibility *without strategy* will guarantee mediocrity—tailoring will be poor, trade-offs nonexistent, fit impossible. All of these require a company to maintain a direction.

What Must Change?

Strategy is a path, not a fixed point. An effective strategy is dynamic. It defines a desired market outcome, not all the means of achieving it. Although continuity of direction is essential to strategy, some kinds of change are absolutely critical to maintaining competitive advantage.

First, you must stay on the frontier of operational effectiveness. If you don't, strategy won't matter. You must continuously assimilate best practices *that do not conflict* with your strategy or the trade-offs essential to it. Failure to keep up on this dimension will result in cost penalties that can swamp your other advantages.

> When you *substitute* flexibility for strategy,
> your organization never stands for anything
> or becomes good at anything.

BMW faced such a challenge in the mid-1990s. Other automakers had invested heavily in best practices. BMW had fallen behind. For example, in product development, BMW could see that its development time of sixty months per vehicle was untenable. It set out to cut the time in half. In the process, BMW embraced a host of important OE improvements, practices that would make *any* automaker more productive regardless of its strategy. For example, the old linear sequence of design tasks was shortened by running some activities in parallel. Crash simulations could be performed on computers instead of with prototypes. These were clear best practices, whether you were producing a luxury sedan or an entry-level family van.

But BMW drew the line where changes might affect the very qualities that make it unique. For example, it implemented a computer-aided styling (CAS) system that took designers about 80 percent to completion, but to achieve BMW's requisite level of styling, the rest needed to be done with physical models. The revised design process was a hybrid that combined the time advantages of CAS with the quality advantages of clay and hand-styling.

With any new technology or management innovation, some uses are going to be best practices that everyone will have to adopt. Other uses will have strategic significance, and you must assess these carefully. The question to ask about any innovation is a simple one: will it reinforce your strategy or will it compromise its uniqueness?

Second, you must change whenever there are ways to extend your value proposition or better ways to deliver it. These changes are strategy specific, and would not benefit all companies equally. To some extent, these opportunities to innovate arise precisely *because* you have a strategy to begin with. Almost from the day CEO Reed Hastings started Netflix to distribute DVDs by mail, he began searching for an Internet-based solution. When it became feasible to stream videos direct to a customer's PC, Netflix saw immediately that doing so would better serve the needs around which its strategy was built in the first place. Mail order was one way of executing its "direct" model. Streaming would further cut the time and the associated logistics costs of shipping DVDs back and forth to a customer's home. (In 2010, the cost, round-trip, for a mailed DVD was about a dollar versus just five cents to stream.) For rivals such as Coinstar's Redbox—whose strategy is built around conveniently located kiosks—the change was less immediately relevant.

Unlike most other automakers, BMW appears to see the coming of electric cars as a way to extend its value proposition. While everyone else is rushing to market using their existing conventional car platforms, BMW engineers are choosing to run their own race. They believe that the only way to achieve the kind of performance and styling for which BMW is known is to design a completely new vehicle from the bottom up. Carbon fiber construction of the passenger compartment and other components will offset the added weight of the car's batteries. According to BMW's design chief, Adrian van Hooydonk, the positioning will be "premium sustainability," aimed at "affluent drivers in urban areas who want to appear environmentally conscious" without having to take a "'rolling vow of poverty.'"

Strategies Emerge and Strategies Evolve

When Porter writes about strategy, he chooses companies with fully developed, rich strategies, companies like Southwest or IKEA. If there were a Nobel Prize for business strategy, these companies would win it. These great exemplars pass all the tests of strategy with flying colors. They have achieved what most managers can only dream of: stellar performance over several decades (figure 7-2). Porter examines those companies, *after the fact*, and asks, What explains their success? The answer is always the same: each was able to create a complex business system elegantly configured to produce a certain kind of value in a specific industry context. Let me underscore that these organizations have spent decades honing these systems, these intricate complex wholes. This is why continuity over time is one of Porter's five tests, and why I call it the enabler.

FIGURE 7-2

Continuity at Southwest Airlines

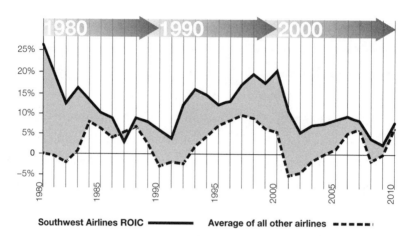

Southwest Airlines ROIC ⸺⸺   Average of all other airlines ▬ ▬ ▬ ▬

Continuity of strategy at Southwest Airlines is reflected in its sustained competitive advantage. Over the 30-year period from 1980 to 2010, Southwests average ROIC was 11.4 percent versus the industry's 3.1 percent. Southwest's advantage was strongest in the 1980s and 1990s. It has been eroding over the past decade in the face of competition from imitators with lower labor costs. At the same time, growth pressures have led Southwest to relax some of its core trade-offs. For example, once it flew only short-haul routes; that's no longer the case. Relaxing trade-offs has economic consequences.

Now, I assume no one is so naive as to believe that Porter is suggesting that anyone can come along and create a Southwest or an IKEA overnight in three easy steps:

1. Do some analysis (five forces, value chain, relative cost and value).

2. Draw an industry map, showing how current players are positioned.

3. Choose an unoccupied position.

Some managers question whether anyone, including Porter himself, could possibly design, in advance, such a complex system. So

maybe doing strategic analysis is a waste of time. Maybe you are better off getting in touch with your inner entrepreneur or unleashing
lots of experiments and seeing what emerges.

So what does Porter say about how to strike the right balance
between designing a strategy analytically and experimenting until one
emerges? You might assume that Porter would come down 100 percent
on the "design" side of the argument. Not so. Good analysis is essential,
but it's a mistake, he argues, to think that a strategy should be fully
defined in its entirety before the fact. There are simply too many variables and too much uncertainty to anticipate everything. Over time, in
the course of serving its customers and vying with its rivals, an organization develops important insights about its strategy that it might not
have had at the start. Over time, new opportunities emerge.

Continuity gives an organization the time it needs to deepen its
understanding of the strategy. Sticking with a strategy, in other words,
allows a company to more fully understand the value it creates and to
become really good at it. Strategies never arrive full-blown and fully
formed on Day One. It took Southwest a full four years after it was
created *even to begin flying*. IKEA's founder, Ingvar Kamprad, started
his company in 1943, but he didn't actually *open a store* until 1958,
and it wasn't until the mid-1960s that IKEA tested its signature self-
service store design. Strategies often emerge through a process of discovery that can take years of trial and error as the company tests its
positioning and learns how best to deliver it.

At the opposite extreme, Porter warns against thinking that an
organization can simply stumble its way into a strategy by encouraging unconnected experimentation in all of its units. Strategy is about
the whole, not the parts. There must be a stable core to begin with, or
at least a grounded hypothesis about how the company is going to
create and capture value.

Often, strategies begin with two or three essential choices. Over
time, as the strategy becomes clearer, additional choices complement

and extend the original ones. Southwest began, as we saw earlier, with three airplanes and the simple value proposition of convenient service at low price. We also saw how important fast gate turnarounds have been to Southwest's competitive advantage. But that crucially important element was not something Southwest's founders figured out in advance.

Early on, CEO Lamar Muse saw an opportunity to provide out-of-state charter service, so he bought a fourth plane. This extra plane also let Southwest add more flights to its regular routes, thus boosting its convenience. As luck would have it, a federal district court then ruled that Southwest could not fly outside the state of Texas. Suddenly the fourth plane was a financial burden. Muse sold it, but he really wanted to maintain the enhanced schedule. It would be possible, but only if they kept gate turnarounds to ten minutes. Necessity became the mother of invention. As one Southwest station manager at the time recalls, "'Most of us, not having an airline background, had no idea that we couldn't do this, so we just did it.'"

When you look at a really good strategy, like Southwest's or IKEA's, the whole is so intricate and consistent, the economic logic so clear and compelling, that you think it *must* have all been planned out in advance. Not so. Consider Dell. The core of its strategy crystallized early around selling direct (avoiding the reseller's margin) and building to order using purchased components (avoiding the cost of internal technology development and component manufacturing). From that core, much developed and changed over time, as the company learned about possibilities inherent in the strategy that Michael Dell didn't envision at the start.

Early on, for example, Dell found that the value proposition was more compelling with larger corporate customers with in-house IT departments than with smaller purchasers. It also turned out that large customers ordered in quantities large enough for Dell to achieve efficiencies in serving them. Thus Dell focused its early efforts on larger corporate customers, leaving what was at the time an unprofitable consumer market for other computer makers.

Years into the strategy, Dell realized that selling direct—and building to customers' orders—gave the company other significant sources of competitive advantage. It resulted in faster cycle times and lower inventory levels, which gave Dell a relative cost advantage at a time when the price of components was falling rapidly. That is, Dell's rivals, having to stock channels, had computers with older, more expensive components. Dell also learned that its direct relationships with its customers gave it better information than its rivals about future demand, and this, in turn, improved its supply chain management. This, up through the early 2000s, was the heart of Dell's cost advantage and its ability to offer its customers standard Windows–Intel technology at lower prices.

It took years for Dell to appreciate fully the economic power of its strategy. The more Dell learned about the importance of inventory to its value proposition, the better it was able to focus everyone in the organization on coming up with new ways to reduce it. While other PC makers tracked their gross margins, Dell kept its eye on ROIC, a measure that highlighted inventory management. And Dell learned from its mistakes as well. Faced with slowing growth in the 1980s, Dell tried to sell through resellers. It quickly did an about-face when it realized that trying to straddle two positions did much more harm than good.

Porter's key point is this: rarely, if ever, is it possible to figure out everything that will eventually matter at the very start. Change, then, is inevitable, and the capacity to change is critically important. But continuity of direction makes effective change more likely. There is no denying that dumb luck has played a role in some extraordinary business successes. But, as Porter likes to ask, would you be eager to invest in someone whose "strategy" is to rely on dumb luck? You may not be able to analyze your way to spectacular success—creativity and serendipity play a role. But armed with an understanding of strategy essentials, you are more likely—far more likely—to make better decisions along the way.

The Continuity Paradox

Since the 1990s, leading change has become the hallmark of a great CEO. The principle of continuity reminds us, however, that not all change is good, that too much change can be bad, and that not all change requires a change in strategy. If you can grasp the role continuity plays in strategy, it will change your thinking about change itself. Paradoxically, continuity of strategy actually improves an organization's ability to adapt to changes in the environment and to innovate.

Paradoxically, continuity of strategy actually improves an organization's ability to adapt to changes and to innovate.

Why? The process of change is about sifting and sorting through massive amounts of information and zeroing in on the actions a company needs to take. Interest and exchange rates fluctuate. Social media grow exponentially. Some new retail format emerges. China does X, India Y. The rising generation exhibits values and work habits different from their parents. Silicon chips achieve incredible circuit density. But clearly, Porter notes, these events, and hundreds of others, are not significant for every company. If you don't have a strategy, then anything and everything could be important. A strategy helps you to decide what's important because you know who you're trying to serve, what needs you're trying to meet, and how your value chain is distinctively configured to do so at the right price. These elements ground a company, enabling it to sort out what matters and what doesn't. Strategy makes priorities clearer. Moreover, if the organization has a purpose that people understand, their willingness to change and their sense of urgency will be higher.

Put in human terms, it is easier to change when you know who you are and what you stand for, and very difficult to change when you don't. It is debilitating for an organization to feel it must serve every new need that emerges or embrace every new technology that comes its way. But when everyone understands the value proposition, an organization can jump at new trends that allow it to be more distinctive in meeting the needs of its customers. It can sift through the sea of changes around it and quickly grasp which ones are relevant. IKEA's hip and educated customer base cares about the environment. IKEA's 2010 catalogue highlights the eco-friendliness of flat packs. IKEA can stay fresh and relevant by marketing an approach that (a) it has been taking for many decades, and (b) is consistent with its low-price strategy.

The deliberate and explicit setting of strategy is *more important than ever* during periods of change and uncertainty.

Organizations are complex. They require time to become really proficient at delivering their chosen kind of value. In what at first sounds like a paradox, Porter argues that the deliberate and explicit setting of strategy is *more important than ever* during periods of change and uncertainty. But it's no paradox at all when you stop to think that strategy offers a clear direction, allowing managers to tune out the many distractions around them. A strategy, with its focus on the spread between customer value and cost, guards against the tendency to follow fads blindly.

Epilogue:

A Short List of Implications

I INTRODUCED THIS BOOK WITH a joke attributed to Mark Twain. Classics, he quipped, are works that everybody wants to have read but nobody wants to read. Now, as I have come to the end, I finally get the point of Twain's joke. It's not that the classics are too hard. It's that we are too lazy and demand too little of ourselves.

What Porter asks of managers is both very simple and very hard. He asks, simply, that managers keep a clear line of sight between their decisions and their performance. But, he says, no cheating allowed—you must be precise and rigorous about it. And unlike most management writers, Porter refuses to tell you what to do. He says, I'll give you guiding frameworks, a general theory that applies in all cases, but the work you do is creative and you have to find your own unique answers.

Management books are notoriously faddish. This year's "groundbreaking" ideas will be of little use three, five, or ten years down the road. But a true classic, to borrow a phrase from the writer Italo

Calvino, is a work "that has never finished saying what it has to say."
Further, "Every rereading of a classic is as much a voyage of discovery
as the first reading."

That has certainly been the case for me. By way of summary, I've
tried to distill into a short list the practical implications of what I've
discovered on rereading Porter. Lists of this sort can easily be trite.
But if you have mastered the essential Porter, you can trace each
implication to the enduring foundation that Porter has built.

Ten Practical Implications

1. Vying to be the best is an intuitive but self-destructive
   approach to competition.

2. There is no honor in size or growth if those are profitless.
   Competition is about profits, not market share.

3. Competitive advantage is not about beating rivals; it's about
   creating unique value for customers. If you have a competitive
   advantage, it will show up on your P&L.

4. A distinctive value proposition is essential for strategy. But
   strategy is more than marketing. If your value proposition
   doesn't require a specifically tailored value chain to deliver it,
   it will have no strategic relevance.

5. Don't feel you have to "delight" every possible customer out
   there. The sign of a good strategy is that it deliberately makes
   some customers unhappy.

6. No strategy is meaningful unless it makes clear what the
   organization will *not* do. Making trade-offs is the linchpin that
   makes competitive advantage possible and sustainable.

7. Don't overestimate or underestimate the importance of good execution. It's unlikely to be a source of a sustainable advantage, but without it even the most brilliant strategy will fail to produce superior performance.

8. Good strategies depend on many choices, not one, and on the connections among them. A core competence alone will rarely produce a sustainable competitive advantage.

9. Flexibility in the face of uncertainty may sound like a good idea, but it means that your organization will never stand for anything or become good at anything. Too much change can be just as disastrous for strategy as too little.

10. Committing to a strategy does not require heroic predictions about the future. Making that commitment actually improves your ability to innovate and to adapt to turbulence.

FAQs:
An Interview with
Michael Porter

This interview was conducted at the Harvard Business School over the course of several sessions during the first quarter of 2011. To prepare, I reviewed transcripts of Professor Porter's speaking events, paying special attention to the questions managers most often raise during the Q&A periods. Those frequently asked questions are reflected here.

I. Common Mistakes and Obstacles

Magretta: What are the most common strategy mistakes you see?

Porter: The granddaddy of all mistakes is competing to be the best, going down the same path as everybody else and thinking that somehow you can achieve better results. This is a hard race to win. So many managers confuse operational effectiveness with strategy.

Another common mistake is confusing marketing with strategy. It's natural for strategy to arise from a focus on customers and their needs. So in many companies, strategy is built around the value proposition, which is the demand side of the equation. But a robust strategy requires a tailored value chain—it's about the supply side as well, the unique configuration of activities that delivers value. Strategy links choices on the demand side with the unique choices about the value chain (the supply side). You can't have competitive advantage without both.

Another mistake is to overestimate strengths. There's an inward-looking bias in many organizations. You might perceive customer service as a strong area. So that becomes the "strength" on which you attempt to build a strategy. But a real strength for strategy purposes has to be something the company can do better than any of its rivals. And "better" because you are performing different activities than they perform, because you've chosen a different configuration than they have.

Another common mistake is getting the definition of the business wrong, or getting the geographic scope wrong. There has been a tendency to define industries broadly, following the influential work of Theodore Levitt some decades ago. His famous example was railroads that failed to see that they were in the transportation business, and so they missed the threat posed by trucks and airfreight. The problem with defining the business as transportation, however, is that railroads are clearly a distinct industry with distinct economics and a separate value chain. Any sound strategy in railroads must take these differences into account. Defining the industry as transportation can be dangerous if it leads managers to conclude that they need to acquire an airfreight company so they can compete in multiple forms of transportation.

Similarly, there has been a tendency to define industries as global when they are national or encompass only groups of neighboring countries. Companies, mindful of the drumbeat about globalization, internationalize without understanding the true economics of their business. The value chain is the principal tool to delineate the geographic boundaries of competition, to determine how local or how global that business is. In a local business, every local area will require a complete and largely separate value chain. At the other extreme, a global industry is one where important activities in the value chain can be shared across all countries.

Reflecting on my experience, however, I'd have to say that the worst mistake—and the most common one—is not having a strategy at all. Most executives think they have a strategy when they really don't, at least not a strategy that meets any kind of rigorous, economically grounded definition.

> The worst mistake—and the most common one—is not having a strategy at all. Most executives think they have a strategy when they really don't.

Magretta: Why is that? Why do so few companies have really great strategies? What are the biggest obstacles to good strategy?

Porter: I used to think that most strategy problems arose from limited or faulty data, or poor analysis of the industry and competitors. To say it differently, I thought the problem was a failure to understand competition. This surely does happen. But the more I have worked in this field, the more I have come to appreciate the more subtle and more pervasive obstacles to clear strategic thinking and how challenging it is for companies to maintain their strategies over time.

There are so many barriers that distract, deter, and divert managers from making clear strategic choices. Some of the most significant barriers come from the many hidden biases embedded in internal systems, organizational structures, and decision-making processes. It's often hard, for example, to get the kind of cost information you need to think strategically. Or the company's incentive system rewards the wrong things. Or human nature makes it really hard to make trade-offs, or to stick with them. The need for trade-offs is a huge barrier. Most managers hate to make trade-offs; they hate to accept limits. They'd almost always rather try to serve more customers, offer more features. They can't resist believing that this will lead to more growth and more profit.

I believe that many companies undermine their own strategies. Nobody does it to them. They do it themselves. Their strategies fail from within.

Then there is the host of strategy killers in the external environment. These range from so-called industry experts to regulators and financial analysts. These all tend to push companies toward what I call "competition to be the best"—the analyst who wants every company to look like the current market favorite, the consultant who helps you benchmark yourself against everyone else in the industry, or who pushes the next big thing, such as the notion that you're supposed to delight and retain every single customer.

Let's take this last idea as an example. If you listen to every customer and do what they ask you to do, you can't have a strategy. Like so many ideas that get sold to managers, there is some truth to it, but the nuances get lost. Strategy is not about making every customer happy. When you've got your strategist's hat on, you want to decide which customers and which needs you want to meet. As to the other customers and the other needs, well, you just have to get over the fact that you will disappoint them, because that's actually a good thing.

I also believe that as capital markets have evolved they have become more and more toxic for strategy. The single-minded pursuit of shareholder value, measured over the short term, has been enormously destructive for strategy and value creation. Managers are chasing the wrong goal.

> Capital markets have become toxic for strategy. The single-minded pursuit of shareholder value . . . has been enormously destructive for strategy and value creation.

These are just some of the obstacles. Cumulatively, they add up. Having a strategy in the first place is hard. Maintaining a strategy is even harder.

Magretta: Would you elaborate on how the capital markets impact strategy?

Porter: This is a multifaceted problem. Let's start with the way financial analysts and the investor community evaluate companies. For any industry, analysts tend to settle on a set of relevant metrics. If it's retailing, for example, it's same-store sales. In another industry, it might be revenue per employee. Of course, it's good to try to find measures that tell you what's going on in a company. But the problem for strategy is that the same metrics are applied to all companies in the industry. One of the important lessons about strategy is that if you're pursuing a different positioning, then different metrics will be relevant. And if you force everybody to show progress on the same metrics, you encourage convergence and undermine strategic uniqueness.

At another level, at any moment in time there's a tendency for the players in the capital markets to identify a "winner." Typically it's the company that seems to be doing well, maybe because it's growing a bit faster, or its profitability the last few quarters has been better. For the analysts, this becomes the gold standard, and then all the companies in the industry are pressured to replicate what the current industry favorite is doing. If the favorite is Pfizer, and Pfizer has been making acquisitions, then everyone else in the industry is pressured to make acquisitions. Follow Pfizer. Do some deals.

Now it often happens that the current favorite eventually falls out of favor, but usually not before the analysts have herded everyone down the same path. And, of course, in strategy there is no one best path. The essence of strategy is to create your own path. You want to run your own race to reach a distinctive endpoint, which is the way you choose to create value. So in this way the capital markets reinforce the mind-set of competition to be the best. And they set themselves up as the arbiter of what "the best" is.

At a third level, the weight of activity in the markets has gravitated toward short-term trading versus long-term investing. People move in and out of stocks quickly, trying to profit from small gaps and discontinuities. But strategy needs a longer time horizon. Building out a unique position in the market takes a series of investments over time. So what are the consequences of this mismatch? If it's going to take a few years to build earnings, but only a few months to buy them, then why not take the quicker path, especially if you can conveniently forget about the intangibles you're writing off after the deal closes. There's a strong bias for doing deals. At the broadest level, then, there's a mismatch between the market's focus on near-term performance and the longer time horizon that would support investment in building a strategic position.

The whole emphasis on shareholder value over the past couple of decades has focused managers on the wrong thing when they should really be focusing on creating economic value sustainably over the long term. The capital markets are better at driving OE, better at keeping pressure on companies to improve efficiency and profitability and to use capital better—these are positive influences. But I have no doubt that the markets damage strategy, even if the impact is subtle and mostly unrecognized.

II. Growth: Opportunities and Pitfalls

Magretta: The capital markets pressure managers to grow. But you've observed that this pressure can have a perverse effect on strategy. How do you grow a business without undermining your strategy?

Porter: This is a huge problem. The pressure to grow is among the greatest threats to strategy. And I'm referring here to growth within a business, not diversification, which is equally challenging. Too often, companies believe that any growth is good growth. They have a tendency to overshoot, by adding product lines, market segments, or geographies that blur uniqueness, create compromises, reduce fit, and ultimately undermine competitive advantage.

The pressure to grow is among the greatest threats to strategy.

My advice is to concentrate on deepening and extending a strategic position rather than broadening and ultimately compromising it. Here are some thoughts about how to grow profitably without destroying your strategy.

First, never copy. Companies always are confronted with opportunities for new products, new services, or moving into adjacent customer groups. How should you think about that? If your competitor has a good idea, learn from it, think about what that innovation accomplishes, but don't just copy it. Figure out how the idea could be adapted and modified in order to reinforce your strategy. Is it relevant to the needs you're trying to serve? Could it be used to reinforce what makes you unique? You don't have to jump on every trend. But if the trend is relevant, tailor it to your strategy.

Second, deepen your strategic position, don't broaden it. A company can usually grow faster—and far more profitably—by better penetrating needs and customers where it is distinctive than by slugging it out in potentially higher growth arenas in which the company lacks uniqueness. So the first place to look for growth is to deepen your penetration of your core target of customers. The common mistake is to settle for 50 percent of your target segment when 80 percent is achievable. You can shoot for true leadership when the customer target is properly defined not as the whole industry, but as the set of customers and needs that your strategy serves best.

Going deeper allows you to leverage all your advantages and improve profitability. Deepening a strategic position in this way involves making the company's activities more distinctive, strengthening fit, and communicating the strategy better to those customers who clearly benefit from what you uniquely do. Gaining 10 percent share in another segment where you have no advantage will often damage your profitability.

Third, expand geographically in a focused way. If you've penetrated your strategic opportunity at home, there's always the rest of the world.

Magretta: Any further advice about tackling foreign markets?
Porter: When you go to a foreign market, remember that you're not trying to serve the whole market. You're looking for the segment *that values what you do*. So when you go to Spain, don't try to compete like existing Spanish companies. Go find those customers who are in your sweet spot. They might not be a big part of the market initially, but can be built up over time. The wonderful thing about geographic expansion is that you can grow with the same strategy. You don't have to serve customers at home whose needs you don't meet very well.

But you have to be really focused, because the tendency in geographic expansion is to get too caught up in the differences present in the new market. Find the part of the new market that responds to what you do rather than try to adapt to all the differences.

Another key characteristic of successful internationalization is that you've got to get direct contact with the customer. It's hard to work through somebody else's distribution channels. You'll never understand the customer needs, you'll never be able to differentiate and distinguish yourself. If somebody else is representing your product and listening to customers, how can you have a strategy?

And be especially careful when making and integrating acquisitions. You buy a Spanish company and all you're going to hear from them is how things are done in Spain. Economists have been studying mergers for twenty years and they find that the seller gets most of the value, not the buyer. Foreign acquisitions must be forcefully repositioned around your strategy, not allowed to continue theirs (unless, of course, theirs is better!).

But geographic expansion can actually be a very powerful way of leveraging and growing your strategy if you do it the right way.

Magretta: And what do you do if none of those approaches to growth are feasible?

Porter: That's an important question that too few managers are willing to face. Sometimes, at the end of the day, the answer is that there are few opportunities to grow rapidly with your strategy and do it profitably. You've got a strong position in your space, and no good way to expand it significantly. Here, the huge mistake is to deny that reality and to try to turn lead into gold. Instead, you should simply make a good ROIC, pay good dividends or otherwise return capital, and enjoy creating value and wealth.

I think many more companies should pay higher dividends rather than take enormous risks trying to grow beyond the capacity of their strategy and their industry structure. Don't set yourself up for failure.

Paying dividends fell out of favor years ago. It became a signal that the management team had no imagination. And that's what gives rise to AOL Time Warner and so many other value-destroying growth plans and deals. The nice thing about dividends is that they're aligned with economic value. You can't pay a dividend unless you create economic value and that's a sign you're actually making good choices about how to compete.

III. Strategy and Innovation

Magretta: Industry boundaries seem to change so fast these days. Does industry really still matter?

Porter: There are two answers to your question, Joan. One is purely empirical. When you look at the data on industry profitability, it tells you that relative profitability differences across industries are remarkably durable. You can look at the data over five years, ten years, even fifteen years, and what you see is that the rank order of industries by their profitability simply doesn't change very much. The airline industry has been down near the bottom of the list for decades. IT software has been up near the top. Those relationships are quite stable. So the data tells us that industry differences are pretty slow to change.

But we also know that industries do undergo structural change and there are discontinuities that sometimes shift industry boundaries and structure in ways that impact profitability. Those things happen. But they are the exception and not the rule. And even when shifts like that do happen, they unfold relatively slowly. The Internet was transformational in changing industry boundaries and structure in a few industries. But even in the Internet space, the great majority of industries were able to embrace the Internet and move on. Even in information-intensive industries like maintenance, repair, and operations distribution, where the Internet was profound, the competitors didn't change, the fundamental structure didn't change.

The second answer to your question about whether industry still matters is this: Even where industry boundaries are changing, the same tools are used to analyze the significance of the change. So the five forces still matter. We have been through a historic period of deregulation, globalization, and technology advances. Some industry boundaries have blurred or shifted. But that doesn't change the fact that every industry has its distinct structure, and its peculiar configuration of the five forces drives the nature of competition in that industry.

You see that one or more of the forces have been significantly affected by some factor—a change on the buyer side, on the supplier side, some discontinuity in the entry barriers, for example. So the same tools apply at any moment in time. If you're trying to understand which trends are going to be important in your industry, look to see how those trends might change some fundamental aspect of structure.

People who believe that industry structure no longer matters are likely to be the same people who see every new technology or management innovation as "disruptive." But you've got to be careful because the data simply doesn't support that view.

Magretta: What is a disruptive technology? Where does it intersect with your thinking about strategy?
Porter: This is a really useful and compelling idea, but it is badly misused and misunderstood to refer to any and every competitive threat. It would be more helpful for managers to use the term only for the far less common situation of real game changers.

A disruptive technology is not any new technology. Many new technologies are not disruptive. Nor is it any big technological leap, because many big leaps are not disruptive. A disruptive technology is one that invalidates value chain configurations and product configurations in ways that allow one company to leap ahead of another and/or make it hard for incumbents to match or respond because of the existing assets they have. So a disruptive technology is one that would invalidate important competitive advantages.

The Internet offers a classic case. It was disruptive where the mechanism for delivering information was fundamental to the product or service, where the business, in essence, was the delivery mechanism. Travel agents, for example, or the recorded music business. But in other cases, the Internet wasn't disruptive because it was simply one more channel for communicating with customers or suppliers. In those cases, established companies with the best product sets and brands were simply able to incorporate the new technology. It wasn't incompatible or inconsistent with anything they were doing.

Two questions will tell you whether you're dealing with a disruptive technology or not. First, to what extent does it invalidate important traditional advantages? Second, to what extent can incumbents embrace the technology without major negative consequences for their business? If you stop and ask those questions, you'll see that true disruptions are not so common. If you look over a decade, for example, at the hundreds of industries that make up the economy, I would guess that less than 5 to 10 percent would be affected by a disruptive technology.

Having said that, managers should of course be on the lookout for potentially disruptive changes. The advice they get tends to focus on just one form of disruption: a simpler and less costly technology is improved and gets good enough to serve a need that's currently met by a more complex and more costly technology. So most managers look for the threat to come from below, from some upstart you've been dismissing as being irrelevant to your business. And then you learn to your horror that for a lot of customers, the upstart is good enough. To use my value proposition terms, the customers' needs were being overserved by the "old" technology. The new one meets just enough of their needs at the right price. Disruption from below is an example of a focus strategy. If you focus on the customers who don't need all the special bells and whistles, you can establish a beachhead. A focuser with a disruptive technology can enter your industry and ultimately grow to occupy a major position. This is the Southwest Airlines story.

But other forms of disruption play a role in strategy. The threat can come from above. You can have an advanced technology or a richer approach that performs at a high level but that can be simplified or streamlined to meet less sophisticated needs at much lower cost. We don't have good evidence on which form is most prevalent, but both exist. Disruptive technology is compelling as a metaphor, but managers need to be rigorous about what's creating the disruption. How does it impact the value chain? Relative price? Relative cost? The strategy fundamentals definitely apply here.

> Disruptive technology is compelling as a metaphor, but managers need to be rigorous about what's creating the disruption.

Magretta: The term "business model" gets a lot of attention in the business press, especially in the context of innovative new businesses. Is a business model the same thing as a strategy?

Porter: The term "business model" is widely used, but it's not precisely defined. So as with the word "strategy," it unfortunately can mean a lot of different things to different people. But here's where I think the concept can be useful. If you're starting a new business and you're not yet sure whether or how it's going to work, the business model concept helps you to focus in on the most basic question of all:

How are we going to make money? What will our costs look like? Where will our revenue come from? How can this business be profitable? There are different ways of getting revenue and different ways of managing costs, and the business model lens can help you to explore those.

But the business model doesn't help you to develop or to assess competitive advantage, which is what strategy aims to do. Strategy goes beyond the basic viability question, *Can we make money?* Strategy asks a more complicated question, How can we make *more* money than our rivals, how can we generate *superior* returns, and then, *How can we sustain that advantage over time?* A business model highlights the relationship between *your* revenues and *your* costs. Strategy goes an important step further. It looks at *relative* prices and *relative* costs, and their sustainability. That is, how your revenues and costs stack up against your rivals'. And then it links those to the activities in your value chain, and ultimately to your income statement and your balance sheet.

So the business model is best used as the most basic step in thinking about the viability of a company. If you're satisfied with just being viable, stop there. If you want to achieve superior profitability (or avoid inferior profitability) and stay viable, then strategy—as I define it—will take you to the next level.

The business model is the most basic step in thinking about the viability of a company. If you're satisfied with just being viable, stop there. If you want to achieve superior profitability, then strategy—as I define it—will take you to the next level.

Magretta: How do you do a five forces analysis if you're an entrepreneur starting a new business in a completely new market space? Is strategy even relevant when there's no existing industry or when conditions are still so fluid that there is no discernible industry structure and no direct competitors?

Porter: Strategy is relevant for any organization at any point in its trajectory. How to develop and sustain a competitive advantage is the core question that every organization has to answer if it's to be successful and to prosper. In emerging industries there's a lot of experimentation. What will the product ultimately look like? What will the distribution system look like? Will the product or service scope produce a stand-alone industry, or will this new idea become part of a larger or existing industry?

There's more uncertainty about the shape of things, but the five forces exercise is fundamentally the same with one big exception: instead of analyzing what already exists, you're forecasting. And you probably know quite a lot about all of the five forces but one. You know the customers you're targeting. Are they likely to be price sensitive? You know who your suppliers are or who they are likely to be. How powerful will they become? You know the substitutes and can identify the likely entry barriers. What you don't have yet are actual rivals. That's where you need to think through who those might be. Will the rivals most likely come from adjacent industries? Or from companies that already exist in other countries? Or will the likely rivals be new start-ups? How would each of these rivals be likely to compete? So even when you're inventing new market space, you probably already know more about the five forces than you realize.

Doing such analysis is important because if you're creating something that's truly valuable, don't kid yourself that no one will follow you. There is no such thing as a market where competition is irrelevant, as nice as that might sound. The idea that innovation allows you to ignore competition is a fairy tale. So you have to have a hypothesis for how the industry might take shape once there is an industry.

Early on, there are many paths the evolution can take, many choices you can make that will have an important impact on how attractive the industry will become. Decisions you and others make over time will begin to lock in the basic economics, making industry structure less fluid. So it's crucial to see different paths for how the industry might evolve, and to ask the basic questions about the five forces, so that you can make choices that will put the industry on the best possible path.

IV. Special Cases: Unattractive Industries, Developing Countries, Nonprofits

Magretta: What if your industry is unattractive? Are you stuck with the five forces, or can you reshape them in your favor?

Porter: The structure of any industry is heavily influenced by some underlying economics. The real profit killer for the airline industry has been the highly unusual combination of low entry barriers and high exit barriers. That's a very rare configuration of forces. So it's not all that hard to start a new airline, but if the company goes out of business, the airplanes don't go away. Airplanes are what we call fungible assets, that is, they can be used by any carrier, on almost any route, at any time. So the plane can change ownership, but the capacity never leaves the market until the plane literally falls apart. If you're running an airline, once you've acquired your planes, hired your staff, and set a schedule, then the fixed costs are enormous and the variable costs are low. Therefore there's intense pressure to fill the plane, and pressure on discounting to do so.

These elements define the underlying economics of the industry and they are reflected in the industry structure. If larger planes have lower operating costs per passenger, that will push the industry toward larger aircraft. That's fundamental economics. Sometimes these basic economics do change. Imagine if someone invented a different kind of airplane engine that changed the economics, that someone lowered the penalty for flying smaller planes. That would relax the economic constraints. That's what happens when you have a new technology that upends the economics.

But some aspects of industry structure result from choices that industry leaders make that lead you down one path or another. There was nothing foreordained in airlines that required the industry to embrace yield management, setting different prices for the identical seat on a flight because of the exact time you bought the ticket. It must have seemed like a smart way to fill seats, but it has, in fact, been a disaster for the industry, creating permanent price competition that has devastated industry profitability. The customer has been trained to shop for the lowest price. Travel sites have emerged to help them do just that. The industry created a profit-devouring monster. Yield management was a choice. It wasn't an inevitable outcome of the industry's economics. So you've got to separate the aspects of industry structure that are truly inherent from those that result from choices you make, choices that could be modified by leadership.

And, stay with me because this is a subtle point, if you are trying to change industry structure, you want to lead the whole industry in a given direction. When you're going for competitive advantage, you're trying to be unique. When you're trying to change the industry structure, you want everyone else to follow you.

Consider how Sysco transformed the food distribution industry. This was an industry with fragmented customers and powerful suppliers, often the big branded food companies. Barriers to entry were low. Rivalry historically had been on price because basically the distributors were all distributing the same products. That's a bad structure. But some of the industry leaders—Sysco, for example—wanted a different kind of competition. They started doing private label to mitigate the power of the suppliers. They ramped up their IT investments, which served as an entry barrier to the small distributors who would be unable to afford those investments. They started to provide value-added services to their customers such as menu and nutrition planning, inventory management, and inventory financing. This shifted competition to dimensions other than price alone. And here, imitation was a good thing. As others followed Sysco's lead, the industry became more attractive.

Magretta: Is strategy important for companies operating in a developing economy? Do the same strategy fundamentals apply?

Porter: Companies in developing economies typically have lower factor costs, such as labor, and this might let them compete for a time with rivals outside the country even if they are behind in OE and their products are not distinctive. But factor cost advantages tend to diminish over time, and eventually companies in developing countries will need to address both of those issues.

First, they have to close the OE gap. They have to overcome deficits in workforce skill levels, technology, and management capabilities. Where companies face a business environment full of obstacles such as poor physical infrastructure and complex regulations, it's a challenge to reach world-class standards in OE and to improve performance in cost and quality.

Second, they have to begin to develop real strategies. Eventually these businesses will have to compete with the multinationals—and it is highly unlikely that a local company will win on operational effectiveness alone. That's a lesson which Guatemala-based Pollo Campero has taken to heart. Pollo Campero competes successfully in the Central American fast food market against giants such as

McDonald's, Burger King, and Pizza Hut. It does so by adapting its value proposition and its value chain to meet local Central American needs. It has also taken the next step, expanding to serve those same needs for a growing Hispanic market in the United States.

Companies in developing economies must eventually transition away from being very reactive and opportunistic to become more strategic, to focus on building a unique position, on developing something distinctive in the market. This means shifting the focus so you're not just relying on a cost advantage, but you're thinking in terms of value, ideally of unique value in the marketplace.

And geographic scope is a real issue. If you look at the data in Turkey, to cite just one example, companies are still much too domestic, much too focused on their own market, even though it is growing. The future is to be international, and that often starts by looking at the region. This often presents a tremendous opportunity, which local companies may be uniquely positioned to serve.

One of the problems I see in developing and emerging economies is that people tend to be too focused on Europe and the United States, and really don't see the opportunity of selling within their region, often because that wasn't possible in the past. The region was closed, and every country was protected, and so the only way you could export was to export out to the advanced economies. But that's changing. There's really a historic opportunity for companies in developing and emerging middle-income economies to start to be international today. Because they can penetrate regional markets, they don't have to penetrate only the advanced markets.

Another problem I see is that companies tend to be very diversified. They still compete in lots of businesses that are very different. It's important to recognize when the time comes to put that model aside, and to move to greater focus in your business groups, where you can put together businesses that can leverage each other, which can enhance your competitive advantage, which can make your position more unique. That's an important transition for companies in emerging economies if they hope eventually to realize their full potential. What has to change is not the quality of the people, but the mind-set, the approach to thinking about how to build a business, in short, about strategy.

Making trade-offs often turns out to be harder for managers in nonprofits.

Magretta: Do nonprofits need strategy? Nonprofits focus a lot on raising money, on their mission, on serving their clients. But they don't spend much time on strategy. Should they? What is strategy for a nonprofit organization?

Porter: Strategy is necessary for any type of organization that serves customers or meets needs. Good strategy for any organization starts with defining appropriate goals. The fundamental goal for a business is superior long-term return on investment. Performance against that goal tells you whether or not the company is creating value. For a nonprofit, there is no directly comparable metric, so you've got to create one. A major challenge for every nonprofit is to define its goal or goals in terms of the social benefits it seeks to create. And then it must develop a value metric that looks at the results achieved versus the costs required to achieve them.

Once the nonprofit has a clear handle on what it's trying to do, then all of the other strategy principles apply. What "customer" are you serving? What's the unique value you will deliver? What needs will you meet? How is your value chain tailored to best serve those needs? Are you making trade-offs with alternative approaches? Do you know what your organization will not do?

Making trade-offs often turns out to be harder for managers in nonprofits. If you don't have clear value metrics to guide you, then it is easy to see almost everything you do as contributing to "good." Because the funder is often not the customer, this can lead to a misalignment between funding and value. Businesses that get paid by customers for what they deliver are powerfully anchored to value. Nonprofits lack that kind of an anchor. Funders, in fact, are sometimes a major source of the distraction. Nonprofits are prone to mission creep when their funders are more willing to support new programs and initiatives than they are to provide operating funding to help you scale what you already do. It's a common strategic challenge facing many nonprofits.

V. Leading the Organization

Magretta: What's your advice on the strategic planning process?
Porter: I am often asked about whether there's a difference between strategic thinking and strategic planning. My answer is that strategic planning should be a process for doing strategic thinking, but it often becomes a time-consuming ritual that really doesn't support strategic thinking at all.

> Strategic planning often becomes a time-consuming ritual that really doesn't support strategic thinking at all.

I think there are a couple of keys to successful strategic planning. One is that you need to bring together the whole team responsible for a particular business, and they need to do the plan together. You can't divide up the work and then try to staple it together at the end. Strategy is about the whole enterprise, not the individual pieces. That's a foundational principle of good strategy. There's no such thing as a good marketing strategy. There's only a good marketing strategy in the context of the overall strategy. The danger with sending people off to do their own functional plans is that you'll end up with a series of unconnected "best practices," not a coherent strategy. That's why a strategic plan needs to involve the whole management team working together to think about the industry, the competitors, the opportunities, the value chain, and then ultimately make some choices about positioning and direction. Then, the team needs to develop the implications for action.

I believe it's beneficial to have a formal strategic planning process because otherwise the day-to-day pressures of the business drive out strategy. There needs to be a process once every year or two, and then quarterly reviews. But you can't let it be simply about budgeting and making guesses about next year's growth rate. Planning needs to support thinking rather than drive it out.

Magretta: How do you get everybody in the organization on the same page?

Porter: Communicating the strategy is really important. Strategy is useless if it's a secret, if nobody else in the organization knows what the strategy is. The purpose of strategy is to align the behavior of everyone in the organization and to help them make good choices when they're on their own. Those choices happen every day—when your salesman is deciding who to call on and what pitch to give, when the folks in product development are thinking about what sort of new ideas to look at. People are out there, every day, making choices. You want them to make the choice that fits the strategy. So you've got to communicate it.

How do you communicate it? Well, you've got to find a concise and memorable way to explain your strategy. Really good leaders crystallize the value proposition into something relatively simple. And then they help individual units in the organization translate what that means for every activity. Good leaders are strategy professors, in the sense that they're teaching strategy all the time. They're giving lots of little talks about strategy. They start every meeting with the twenty-fifth repetition of the essence of the value proposition. Then it goes on to whatever the meeting is about. The employee dialogues always start with, What do we stand for as a company? What makes us distinctive? How are we unique? And it goes on from there. You're constantly repeating and you're encouraging your direct reports to also give the same speech to their organizations. It's important, if you're the general manager, to sit in on some of those meetings where your direct reports are trying to explain the strategy, and listen to see how they do, just to make sure that people really understand it.

I've seen too many organizations where the understanding of the strategy and the agreement about it are superficial. Everyone can agree at some very high level, but then when you get into the detail, you see that people actually don't understand, and they don't agree. They act at cross-purposes to each other. So you've got to create an opportunity to really understand the way people think and to confront the issues.

I also believe that you should communicate your strategy to your customers, to your suppliers, to your channels, and to the capital markets. You've got to help the capital markets understand how you're going to be superior and what metrics they ought to be using to see, first of all, how you're superior and how you're progressing in your strategy. Don't assume that stock analysts will figure it out. You've got to tell them.

If your competitor hears you give a speech about your strategy, so much the better. Because if you have a clear strategy with trade-offs and choices, the more the competitor knows you're committed to it, the more likely they are to do something else, to avoid head-to-head competition where they're not going to be able to win. Ultimately, I think communicating widely is the only way to do it. Now you don't necessarily want to tell your competitor which machine you're going to buy and when you're going to introduce a new product and all the details that might give them some ability to make things difficult for you. But the basic direction you're going is something else. They're going to find out anyway, so you might as well communicate it clearly in your own words.

And finally, if there are individuals who don't accept the strategy, who simply refuse to get on board, they cannot have an ongoing role in the company. That's a polite way of saying they've got to go. You can't debate strategy among yourselves for very long. You just can't. It's too hard to implement well even with a willing management team. I've seen too many cases where executives just let the dissenters hang on. The resulting negative energy and confusion and waste of time really damage the strategy. It's healthy for people to disagree and managers should be given a chance to make their case and to change minds, but there comes a time when the discussion has to end. It's not about democracy, or consensus, or about making everyone happy. Fundamentally, it's about picking a direction and then getting every-body really excited about it.

A Porter Glossary:
Key Concepts

activities: Discrete economic processes, such as operating a sales force, developing products, or physical delivery to the customer. An activity usually involves people, technology, fixed assets, sometimes working capital, and various types of information. The activities companies perform are the basic units of competitive advantage because they are the ultimate source of both relative costs and the levels of differentiation a company can offer its customers.

barriers to entry: The hurdles a new entrant would have to surmount in order to enter an industry. Low entry barriers (i.e., industries that are easy to enter) lower the industry's average profitability. The threat of new entrants is one of the five forces.

barriers to imitation: The hurdles facing a rival within an industry who tries to move from one positioning to another in order to copy another company's strategy. Barriers to imitation slow the process of competitive convergence.

clusters: Geographic concentrations of companies, suppliers, related industries, and specialized institutions such as academic programs— think Hollywood (entertainment), for example, Silicon Valley (technology), or Seurat, India (diamond cutting). Clusters play an important role in competition because a company's productivity is influenced by the presence of like firms, institutions, and infrastructure around it. With effective local suppliers of time-sensitive services, for example, a company will be more efficient. Clusters draw on local assets and institutions, such as public education, physical infrastructure, clean water, fair competition laws, quality standards, and transparency. Clusters are prominent features of all successful and growing economies, and a crucial driver of competitiveness, entrepreneurship, and new business growth. For more on this topic, see "Clusters and Competition" in Porter's *On Competition* (2008).

competition: The term is commonly used to refer to rivals and rivalry, but for Porter, this definition is too narrow. Competition is the tug-of-war over profits that occurs not just between rivals but also between a company and its customers, its suppliers, makers of substitutes, and potential new entrants.

competitive advantage: The term is commonly used to mean "Here's what we think we're good at," as in "Our competitive advantage is technology." Or, it is used even more loosely, as in "Our competitive advantage lies in our people." Porter's definition is tightly linked to the economics of competition: you have competitive advantage if your profitability is sustainably higher than that of your rivals. Then you can dig further to understand whether that advantage comes from higher prices, lower costs, or some combination of both. These differences in relative price or relative costs arise because of *differences in the activities* being performed.

competitive convergence: What happens when companies imitate and match each other's moves, when they compete to be the best. Over time all companies begin to look alike as one difference after another erodes. When rivals converge around a standard offering, customers must choose on price alone. Mainstream economics has always highlighted the way in which this kind of "perfect" competition benefits customers by lowering prices. But Porter sees it differently. Convergence can actually hurt customers because it limits their choice.

competitiveness (of a nation, a location): The term is commonly used to describe a region or country with low-cost labor or some other conventional comparative advantage such as access to a valuable natural resource. In Porter's view, the focus on low-cost inputs, on "comparative advantage," is far less relevant than it once was. Porter defines the competitiveness of a location in terms of how productively it uses its human and natural resources as well as its capital. Competitiveness arises, in other words, from how well a location *uses* inputs to produce valuable goods and services, not from the inputs it *has*. It arises from choices, not endowments. Moreover, Porter argues that the productivity and prosperity possible in a given location depend not on *what industries* its firms compete in, but on *how* they compete. Policy makers and executives, through their choices, create a business environment that affects how companies compete, and thus their competitiveness. For more on this topic, see "The Competitive Advantage of Nations" in *On Competition* (2008).

competitor analysis: Intelligence gathering and analysis aimed at helping a company deal with competitive dynamics by assessing the intentions and capabilities of rivals. For more on this topic, see Porter's seminal work in chapter 3 of *Competitive Strategy* (1980).

continuity: Porter uses the term to refer to stability in the core value proposition. It is his fifth test of a good strategy. A strategy is a path, not a destination. A company can stay on the path without standing still, a distinction that is misunderstood by those who think that strategy is somehow "static," or that it doesn't allow for change. All of the other elements of strategy—tailoring a value chain to the value proposition, extending trade-offs, achieving fit across activities—take time to develop. Without continuity of direction, a company would be unable to develop and deepen its competitive advantage.

corporate strategy: The overall strategy for a corporation that consists of diversified businesses in multiple industries; it is *not* the same thing as a competitive strategy. Because competitive advantage is won or lost at the level of an individual business, the goal of corporate strategy should be to enhance the competitive advantage of its multiple business units. But because the corporation sits "on top" of the business units and is the seat of power and control, this distinction is often lost in practice. The cart often leads the horse, giving corporate "synergy" a bad name. For more on this topic, see "From Competitive Advantage to Corporate Strategy" in Porter's *On Competition* (2008).

cost driver: The factors that influence cost. In analyzing a company's cost position, look at each distinct activity to see which factors influence the cost of that activity. *Competitive Advantage* (1985) has a fifty-page chapter on this important subject.

diamond theory: A major Porter framework (not covered in this book) that explains why some nations and regions achieve greater economic success in a given industry than others. *Comparative advantage* attributes a region's success to low-cost labor or access to a valuable natural resource. In contrast, Porter highlights the role of *competitive advantage*, achieved through higher productivity and innovation. These arise, according to diamond theory, where the local environment is the most forward-looking, dynamic, and challenging. See *The Competitive Advantage of Nations* (1990).

differentiation: The term is most commonly used simply to mean "different." In marketing, it is used to describe how one offering is positioned in relation to others (i.e., it might offer more quality or features, or it might sell at a lower price). Porter uses this term more narrowly to refer to a company's ability to command a higher relative price than rivals because its offering has increased customers' willingness to pay. Porter prefers this narrower and more precise definition because he believes it is essential not to confuse the two components of competitive advantage: price and cost.

diversification: The expansion of a company into different businesses. Porter's thinking about diversification is directly linked to the value chain and its activities. Too often, Porter observes, core competences that are vaguely defined provide a rationale for diversification that turns out to be in businesses that are actually unrelated. The challenge in diversification is to identify activities or activity systems that can be shared with new businesses, or to find businesses where your proprietary skills in managing specific activities can be transferred. This is how valuable resources or competences can be leveraged. For more on this topic, see "From Competitive Advantage to Corporate Strategy" in Porter's *On Competition* (2008).

execution: See *operational effectiveness (OE)*.

fit: When the value or cost of one activity is affected by the way other activities are performed. One of the five basic tests of a good strategy, fit can amplify the value of a competitive advantage by lowering costs or by producing unique value that raises a customer's willingness to pay. It also amplifies the sustainability of a strategy, making it harder for rivals to understand and copy the strategy's complex system of activities.

five forces: Porter's seminal framework for assessing competition in any industry by analyzing the industry's structure. The framework explains the large and sustained differences in profitability from one industry to another. Five forces analysis is the first step in thinking about strategy, about how to shift the forces in your favor, and where you might be able to establish a unique positioning. For the framework and an extensive application of it, see "The Five Competitive Forces That Shape Strategy" and "Strategy and the Internet" in Porter's *On Competition* (2008).

frameworks: The term Porter uses to distinguish his approach from formal economic models. Formal models can capture only those aspects of competition that can be represented and solved mathematically, and this requires sharply limiting the number of variables that can be considered. Porter's frameworks accept that competition is too complex to lend itself to formal modeling; they are more like expert systems that help you to consider the relevant dimensions of competition.

generic strategies: Broad characterizations of the key themes of strategic positioning. A focused strategy chooses to limit the scope of customers and needs that a company serves. A differentiation strategy allows a company to command a premium price, while cost leadership allows it to compete by offering a low relative price. The idea of generic strategies was a seminal concept first described by Porter in *Competitive Strategy* (1980) and has been widely embraced by managers ever since. Effective strategies typically integrate multiple themes in a unique way. You can be differentiated in some ways *and* be low cost, for example, as long as the particular kind of differentiated value is not inconsistent with low costs. See *stuck in the middle*.

geographic scope: For strategy, it is critical to draw the geographic boundaries of your industry correctly. Is your business global, national, regional, or local? Significant differences in the five forces suggest that you may be dealing with separate industries. There has been a tendency, Porter notes, to define businesses as being global when in fact there are significant differences in industry structure from one country or region to the next that would demand different strategies. See "Competing Across Locations: Enhancing Competitive Advantage Through a Global Strategy" in *On Competition* (2008).

global strategy, globalization: See *geographic scope*.

industry structure: The basic, underlying economic and technological characteristics of an industry that shape the competitive arena in which strategy must be set. Analyzing industry structure is the place to start in order to understand the competitive environment as well as the profit potential of the industry. See *five forces*.

operational effectiveness (OE): Commonly called "best practice" or "execution" by managers, OE is Porter's umbrella term for a company's ability to perform the same or similar activities better than rivals. OE includes a multitude of practices that allow a company to get more out of the resources it uses. Every functional area has its current best practices: the best way to load a factory, the best way to train a sales force, and so on. Differences in OE are pervasive and can explain some differences in relative profitability. OE is about achieving excellence in execution. OE is important to performance, but it is different from strategy. For more on OE, see "What Is Strategy?" in Porter's *On Competition* (2008).

outsourcing: The decision to buy from a third party an activity that your organization once performed internally. The received wisdom has been to retain those activities that are "core" and to outsource the rest. Porter offers a different way to frame the decision, linking it directly to the economics of competitive advantage: retain those functions that are or could be tailored to your strategy, and outsource those that are truly generic, for which little tailoring is possible or relevant to the strategy.

Porter hypothesis: The name given by the environmental community to Porter's argument that corporate pollution is often a sign of economic waste: of resources used inefficiently, energy wasted, or valuable raw materials discarded. Improving environmental performance, then, will often increase productivity and, in some cases, even offset the cost of making improvements. Corporations therefore should see environmental improvement not as a regulatory nuisance but as an essential part of improving productivity and competitiveness. Smart environmental regulation, Porter argues, encourages product and process innovation. See Porter's article (with Claas van der Linde) "Green and Competitive: Ending the Stalemate" in *On Competition* (2008).

positioning: The choice of a value proposition made against a specific and relevant set of industry rivals. Discovering a good strategy means finding a unique positioning, the "place" you want to be in your industry.

relative buyer value: How much the customer is willing to pay for a good or service versus other offerings.

relative cost: Your cost per unit relative to that of your rivals. A relative cost advantage can come from two possible sources: performing the same activities better (competing to be the best, or OE) or choosing to perform different activities (competing to be unique).

relative price: Your price per unit relative to that of your rivals. A relative price advantage comes from differentiation that produces buyer value, or in plainer English, from producing something distinctive for which customers are willing to pay more.

return on invested capital (ROIC): A financial measure that weighs the profits a business generates versus the capital invested in it. For Porter, this is the best financial measure of success because it captures how effectively a company uses its resources to generate economic value.

strategic competition: Porter uses this term to refer to positive-sum competition, in which companies win (and achieve superior profitability) by creating unique value for their customers. This is a win–win form of competition because your customers benefit and so do you.

strategy: The word is commonly used to refer to any important goal or initiative, as in "Our strategy is to be number 1 in our industry," or "Our strategy is to grow through acquisitions." Porter's definition: the set of integrated choices that define how you will achieve superior performance in the face of competition. It's not the goal (e.g., be number 1), nor is it a specific action (e.g., make acquisitions). It's the positioning you choose that will result in achieving the goal; the actions are the path you take to realize the positioning. Moreover, when Porter defines strategy, he is really talking about what constitutes a *good* strategy, one that will result in a higher ROIC than the industry average.

stuck in the middle: A Porter phrase that quickly became part of the strategy lexicon to describe a strategic trap companies fall into when they refuse to make trade-offs, when they try to be all things to all customers. The problem is that when you try to offer types of value that are inconsistent, you will inevitably fail to be as efficient or effective as a more focused competitor that has been willing to tailor its activities to deliver that unique value.

substitute: A product from another category that a customer might choose to meet the same need your product serves. To the dismay of traditional watchmakers, cellphones are becoming a substitute for wristwatches, especially for the younger generation. The threat of substitutes is one of the five forces.

SWOT analysis: A simple and widely used tool developed in the 1960s to organize discussions in strategic planning meetings. Managers are asked to list the company's strengths, weaknesses, opportunities, and threats (SWOT). SWOT attempts to relate a company to its environment, but it is typically short on analysis and objectivity. SWOT predates the insights that derive from Porter's work.

tailored value chain: Porter uses the word "tailored" to refer to activities that are designed specifically to deliver a certain value proposition. A tailored activity is the opposite of a generic one. Having a tailored value chain is Porter's second test of a good strategy.

trade-offs: Trade-offs occur when companies have to makes choices between strategic positionings that are inconsistent. Those kinds of choices give rise to differences among rivals in cost and value, and thus trade-offs are the economic linchpin of strategy. One of the five tests of good strategy, trade-offs contribute to the cost and price differences that constitute competitive advantage. Trade-offs also make it difficult for rivals that have made different choices to copy what you do without damaging their own strategies. Thus, trade-offs make competitive advantage sustainable by deterring imitation from existing rivals.

value chain: The set of all the discrete activities a firm performs in creating, producing, marketing, and delivering its good or service. This is the basic tool for understanding competitive advantage, since all costs arise from the value chain's activities and all differentiation is created by them.

value creation: The process by which organizations transform inputs into goods and services that are worth more than the sum of those inputs. This is the ultimate source of superior performance for businesses that exist to create economic value, and for nonprofits that exist to meet a specific social objective with the greatest efficiency. Strategy is about how any organization will create unique value for its chosen customers.

value proposition: The core element of strategy that defines the kind of value a company will create for its customers. A value proposition answers three questions: Which customers are you going to serve? Which needs are you going to meet? What relative price will you charge? A unique value proposition is the first test of a good strategy.

value system: The full set of end-to-end activities involved in creating value for the end user. A company's value chain is typically just a

part of a larger value system that includes companies either upstream
(suppliers) or downstream (distribution channels), or both. This perspective about how value is created forces you to consider every activity in the process, regardless of who performs that activity. It also
forces you to see each activity not just as a *cost*, but as a step that has
to add some increment of value to the finished product or service. In
thinking about your own value chain, then, it's important to see how
your activities have points of connection with those of your suppliers,
channels, and customers.

zero-sum competition: A form of rivalry in which you win only if
someone else loses, even if the "someone else" is your customer or
your supplier. For example, Porter's description of U.S. health-care
competition: "Costs are reduced by shifting them to others. Physicians are pressured to improve productivity by skimping on time
spent with patients. Physicians win by cutting better deals with their
hospitals . . . Hospitals win by merging into groups to gain more bargaining clout on rates . . . Health plans win by restricting services and
muscling physicians to accept lower pay. In ways such as these, each
player in the system gains not by increasing value for the patient but
by taking value away from someone else." See Porter and E. Teisberg,
"How Physicians Can Change the Future of Health Care," *JAMA*
297, no. 10 (2007).

Chapter Notes
and Sources

For a comprehensive bibliography of Porter's work, including presentations and interviews, see the Web site of the Institute for Strategy and Competitiveness, http://isc.hbs.edu. To help readers pursue particular topics of interest, I have referenced a number of Porter's published works in the glossary.

Introduction

Porter described the intellectual divide he faced in the 1970s in a private conversation with me in the fall of 2010. His reflections on the origins of his frameworks appear in M. E. Porter, N. Argyres, and A. M. McGahan, "An Interview with Michael Porter," *Academy of Management Executive* 16, no. 2 (2002): 43–52.

Chapter 1. Competition: The Right Mind-Set

The airport seating example was suggested by Daniel Michaels, "Hot Seat: Airport Furniture Designers Battle for Glory," *Wall Street Journal*, May 17, 2010. The hotel bed wars quote was reported by Christopher Elliott, "Détente in the Hotel Bed Wars," *New York Times*, January 31, 2006. See also Youngme Moon, "The Hotel Bed Wars," Case 9-509-059 (Boston: Harvard Business School, 2009).

Chapter 2. The Five Forces: Competing for Profits

This chapter draws from and quotes Michael E. Porter's "The Five Competitive Forces That Shape Strategy," reprinted in *On Competition, Updated and Expanded Edition* (Boston: Harvard Business School Publishing, 2008).

The story of market power in the cement industry comes from Peter Fritsch, "Hard Profits: A Cement Titan in Mexico Thrives by Selling to Poor," *Wall Street Journal*, April 22, 2002. See also Pankaj Ghemawat, "The Globalization of CEMEX," Case 9-701-017 (Boston: Harvard Business School, 2004).

The "receipt and dispatch" work rule is described by Micheline Maynard, "More Than Money Is at Stake in Votes by Airline Unions," *New York Times*, April 29, 2003.

For an example of an extremely thorough and rigorous five forces analysis, see the posting on the ISC Web that covers the airline industry, at http://www.isc.hbs.edu/pdf/IATA_Vision_2050_Chapter_1.pdf. For help with doing your own industry analysis, see Jan Rivkin and Ann Cullen, "Finding Information for Industry Analysis," Note 9-708-481 (Boston: Harvard Business School, 2010).

Chapter 3. Competitive Advantage: The Value Chain and Your P&L

The Kelleher quote about profits comes from Kevin and Jackie Freiberg, *Nuts! Southwest Airlines' Crazy Recipe for Business and Personal Success* (Austin, TX: Bard Press, 1996), 49. This is an engaging, insightful account of the early history of Southwest that I draw upon again in later chapters.

My value chain template is a simplified version of Porter's classic graphic. For the original, see Chapter 2 of *Competitive Advantage: Creating and Sustaining Superior Performance* (New York: Free Press, 1985) and also "How Information Gives You Competitive Advantage," reprinted in *On Competition* (2008). For a great lesson in how to use value chain analysis, see Porter and Robert S. Kaplan, "How to Solve the Cost Crisis in Health Care," *Harvard Business Review*, September 2011.

I first learned about Whirlwind Wheelchair from the PBS Frontline/World documentary *Wheels of Change*, produced by Marjorie McAfee and Victoria Gamburg, reported by Marjorie McAfee. Whirlwind's Executive Director, Marc Krizack, provided me with valuable insights about his organization in a series of private exchanges in April 2011.

Three excellent sources for help with the analytics of competitive advantage (topics such as relative cost, cost drivers, and willingness to pay) are the following:

- Pankaj Ghemawat and Jan W. Rivkin, "Creating Competitive Advantage," Note 9-798-062 (Boston: Harvard Business School, 2006).

- Hanna Halaburda and Jan W. Rivkin, "Analyzing Relative Costs," Note 9-708-462 (Boston: Harvard Business School, 2009).

- Tarun Khanna and Jan Rivkin, "Math for Strategists," Note 9-705-433 (Boston: Harvard Business School, 2005).

I have written about Dell, Honda, and Schwab in *What Management Is: How It Works and Why It's Everyone's Business* (New York: Free Press, 2002).

For the Nomacorc example, see Timothy Aeppel, "Show Stopper: How Plastic Popped the Cork Monopoly," *Wall Street Journal*, May 1, 2010.

Porter argues against confusing OE with strategy in "What Is Strategy?" reprinted in *On Competition* (2008).

For an analysis of Japan's competitive problems, see Michael E. Porter, Hirotaka Takeuchi, and Mariko Sakakibara, *Can Japan Compete?* (Cambridge, MA: Perseus Publishing, 2000).

Chapter 4. Creating Value: The Core

The Porter quotes and concepts in this chapter, as well as his analysis of Southwest Airlines, come from "What Is Strategy?" reprinted in *On Competition* (2008). The graphic depicting the value proposition is Porter's, derived from unpublished presentation materials.

Details of Southwest's early pricing and its expansion come from *Nuts!*, cited earlier.

I have written about Walmart, Enterprise, Southwest, and Aravind in *What Management Is* (2002), and on Walmart in "Why Business Models Matter," *Harvard Business Review*, May 2002.

For more on Aravind, see V. Kasturi Rangan, "The Aravind Eye Hospital, Madurai, India: In Service for Sight," Case 9-593-098 (Boston: Harvard Business School, 2009).

My source for Progressive is John Wells, Marina Lutova, and Ilan Sender, "The Progressive Corporation," Case 9-707-433 (Boston: Harvard Business School, 2008).

A good article on Enterprise is Carol Loomis, "The Big Surprise Is Enterprise," *Fortune*, July 14, 2006.

For Edward Jones, I have used David J. Collis and Michael G. Rukstad, "Can You Say What Your Strategy Is?" *Harvard Business Review*, April 2008; and David J. Collis and Troy Smith, "Edward Jones in 2006: Confronting Success," Case 9-707-497 (Boston: Harvard Business School, 2009).

My source for the history of Grace Manufacturing is John T. Edge, "How the Microplane Grater Escaped the Garage," *New York Times*, January 11, 2011.

Chapter 5. Trade-offs: The Linchpin

This chapter draws on unpublished research on McDonald's, British Airways' Go Fly, Home Depot, and Lowe's done by Andrew Funderburk, an alumnus of Porter's Institute for Strategy and Competitiveness. See also Stephanie Clifford, "Revamping, Home Depot Woos Women," *New York Times*, January 28, 2011.

Porter's analysis of IKEA comes from "What Is Strategy?" reprinted in *On Competition* (2008). For the research showing that people value more highly something they build themselves, see Michael I. Norton, Daniel Mochon, and Dan Ariely, "The 'IKEA Effect': When Labor Leads to Love," working paper 11-091, Harvard Business School, Boston, 2011.

I first learned about In-N-Out Burger from Youngme Moon's *Different: Escaping the Competitive Herd* (New York: Crown Business, 2010). The company's history is nicely told by Stacy Perman, *In-N-Out Burger: A Behind-the-Counter Look at the Fast-Food Chain That Breaks All the Rules* (New York: Harper Collins, 2009).

Chapter 6. Fit: The Amplifier

Porter writes about the types of fit in "What Is Strategy?" reprinted in *On Competition* (2008).

Two excellent sources on Zara are Kasra Ferdows, Michael A. Lewis, and Jose A. D. Machucam, "Rapid-Fire Fulfillment,"*Harvard Business Review*, November, 2004; and Pankaj Ghemawat and José Luis Nueno, "Zara: Fast Fashion," Case 9-703-497 (Boston: Harvard Business School, 2003).

The quotation from Reed Hastings about Netflix's matching problem comes from William C. Taylor and Polly LaBarre, *Mavericks at Work: Why the Most Original Minds in Business Win* (New York: HarperCollins, 2006).

Roger Martin blogged about AT&T's value destruction in "When Strategy Fails the Logic Test," November 24, 2010, http//blogs.hbr.org/martin/2010/11/i-pretty-much-knew-that.html.

Chapter 7. Continuity: The Enabler

Porter applies five forces thinking to the analysis of potentially disruptive technologies in "Strategy and the Internet," reprinted in *On Competition* (2008).

For Nestlé's milk business, see Porter and Mark R. Kramer, "Strategy and Society: The Link Between Competitive Advantage and Corporate Social Responsibility," reprinted in *On Competition* (2008).

The Sears story is told by Roger Hallowell and James I. Cash Jr., "Sears, Roebuck and Company (A): Turnaround," Case 898-007 (Boston: Harvard Business School, 2002).

Alan Mulally's remarks about Ford's transformation are reported by Bill Vlasic, "Ford's Bet: It's a Small World After All," *New York Times*, January 10, 2010.

This account of BMW's design process is from S. Thomke, "Managing Digital Design at BMW," *Design Management Journal* 12, no. 2 (2001).

Good sources for Netflix are Michael V. Copeland, "Reed Hastings: Leader of the Pack," *Fortune*, November 18, 2010; and Willy Shih, Stephen Kaufmann, and David Spinola, "Netflix," Case 9-607-138 (Boston: Harvard Business School, 2009).

For BMW's thinking on its electric car, see Jack Ewing, "Latest Electric Car Will Be a BMW, From the Battery Up," *New York Times*, July 1, 2010.

The story of how Southwest's fourth plane led to ten-minute gate turns is told in *Nuts!*, 33–34.

I have written about Dell in *What Management Is* (2002) and in "Why Business Models Matter," *Harvard Business Review*, May 2002; and I interviewed Michael Dell in "The Power of Virtual Integration," *Harvard Business Review*, March 1998. For more on Dell, see Jan W. Rivkin and Michael E. Porter, "Matching Dell," Case 9-799-158 (Boston: Harvard Business School, 1999).

Nicolaj Siggelkow has written about Liz Claiborne in "Change in the Presence of Fit," *Academy of Management Journal* 44 (2001): 838–857.

The quote about the importance of strategy in turbulent times comes from Michael E. Porter and Jan W. Rivkin, "Industry Transformation," Note 701-008 (Boston: Harvard Business School, 2000).

Index

About the Author

Joan Magretta's collaboration with Michael Porter began almost two decades ago, when she was the strategy editor at *Harvard Business Review*. She has worked closely with Porter on many publications, including two of his most influential articles: "What Is Strategy?" and "The Five Competitive Forces That Shape Strategy." She is currently a Senior Associate at Porter's Institute for Strategy and Competitiveness at Harvard Business School.

Magretta is known for her writing about strategy and general management. In 1998 she won the McKinsey Award, given each year for the best article to appear in HBR. Her most recent book, *What Management Is: How It Works and Why It's Everyone's Business* (2002), appears in fifteen languages. It was praised by the *Financial Times* for its refreshing clarity and named one of the three best business and economics books of the year by *The Economist*, which described it as "A rare animal—a management book that is lucid, interesting, and honest." It was also chosen for *BusinessWeek*'s top ten list, cited as a much needed "road map back to business basics."

Prior to joining HBR, Magretta was a partner at Bain & Co. Over the course of her career, she has advised senior management in a wide range of settings—from health care to high fashion, from heavy manufacturing to higher education.

Before getting her MBA at Harvard Business School in 1983, Magretta was a professor in the humanities, teaching literature and film. She is a Phi Beta Kappa graduate of the University of Wisconsin, with an MA from Columbia and a PhD in English from the University of Michigan.